BREADLINE USA

BREADLINE USA

The Hidden Scandal of American Hunger and How to Fix It

Sasha Abramsky

 PoliPointPress

Lyrics from Marc Blitzstein's *The Cradle Will Rock* (1936) used by permission of the Blitzstein estate.

Portions of this book appeared in a slightly different form in *In These Times*: "Blue Collar, Bare Cupboards," March 26, 2008. In These Times, 2040 North Milwaukee Avenue, Chicago, IL 60647. *The Nation*: "Running on Fumes," October 17, 2005; "Reversing Right to Work," October 27, 2006; and "The Moral Minimum," November 6, 2006. The Nation, 33 Irving Place, New York, NY 10003. *The Progressive*: "Is Idaho the Future?" September, 2005. The Progressive, 409 East Main Street, Madison, WI 53703. *Sacramento News & Review*: "America's Dirtiest Secret," February 15, 2007, and "Stagflation," April 24, 2008. Sacramento News & Review, 1015 20th Street, Sacramento, CA 95811. All rights reserved.

Production management: BookMatters
Book design: BookMatters
Cover design: Naylor Design

The Library of Congress catalogued the first edition of this book as follows:

Abramsky, Sasha.
    Breadline USA : the hidden scandal of American hunger / Sasha Abramsky.
        p.   cm.
    Includes index.
    ISBN 978-19362270-9-9 (pbk)
    1. Hunger—United States. I. Title.
    RA601.A27   2009
    363.80973—dc22   2009006799

Published by:
PoliPointPress, LLC
80 Liberty Ship Way, Suite 22
Sausalito, CA 94965
(415) 339-4100
www.p3books.com

Distributed by Ingram Publisher Services

Printed in the USA

Contents

14.95

To my daughter Sofia and my son Leo.

I love you both more than words can say.
May you grow up in a world where all children
have the chance to experience the same insane joy
that you get when eating ice cream or chocolate cake.
May the world you inherit be fairer and friendlier
than the one you were born into.

Acknowledgments

Though most of the reporting in these pages was done specifically for this book, in places I have borrowed either language or concepts from articles I published on economic themes over the past half decade. Thanks to the editors at the *Nation*, *Mother Jones*, the *Progressive*, *In These Times*, the *Sacramento News & Review*, and the UK's *Guardian* newspaper for understanding the importance of poverty in modern-day America and for commissioning these pieces.

I am deeply indebted to the hundreds of people who shared their stories with me; took me into hidden communities; at times, translated for me; helped me gather and interpret economic, hunger, and health-care data; and worked with me to navigate America's complex food distribution paths. Were I to name you all individually, the list would run to many pages. I do, however, owe particular debts of gratitude to Dean Baker, Bob Pollin, and Jose Garcia for talking me through some of the more complex economic themes that show up in my book; to Amy Block Joy for the generosity with which she shared her expertise and scholarship; to Graciella Martinez, Edie Jessup, Liz Tate, Zack Wilson, Royce Wright, Kathy Gardner, and George and Billy MacPherson for welcoming me into their communities and helping link me up with food pantry clients; to Blake

Young, executive director of the Sacramento Food Bank, for tolerating my numerous phone calls, welcoming me into the food bank as a volunteer, and accepting my intrusive journalistic presence on both sides of the food pantry windows.

While time and space constraints prevent me from telling as many stories, from as many parts of the country, as I would like, the information sent my way by individuals and groups from around the United States has helped me, I hope, to paint a comprehensive picture of the growing difficulties faced by America's poor and hungry in all corners of the land. I started work on this mural when the country as a whole was still enjoying flush times. I finished with the country sinking into its worst financial and economic crisis in three-quarters of a century. As conditions changed, so the timbre of my work shifted. Gathering storm clouds increasingly darkened the landscape I was describing. Gary Dymski, at the University of California Center in Sacramento (UCCS), spent hours brainstorming with me about the changing economic and political climate of the country; so, too, did A.G. Block, Art Amos, John Griffing, Jock O'Connell, and many other UCCS staffers and visitors.

Thanks to the staff at Demos, in New York, for making me a senior fellow, and for continuing to link me up with resources and contacts throughout this writing journey, and to my colleagues in the University Writing Program at the University of California at Davis for their ongoing interest in, and support for, my writing.

To my journalistic friends with whom I have shared ideas, laughter, and many beers over the years. To Eyal Press, Adam Shatz, George Lerner, Rose George, Maura McDermott, Steve Magagnini, John Hill, Carolyn Juris, Kim Gilmore, Silja Talvi, and Theo Emery. To Raj Patel, a fellow Balliol College, Oxford alumnus, whose book *Stuffed and Starved* did so much to bring the topic of global hunger to the forefront of political conversation. To Jason Ziedenberg for making every Thanksgiving a noteworthy one. And to Dave

Colburn for his wonderful insights and his generous help over the years with my Web site.

For their confidence in the worth of this project, and their support in bringing an idea from its inchoate origins through to its publication, thanks to my agent Victoria Skurnick, and to Peter Richardson, my always empathetic editor at PoliPointPress. Your enthusiasm has, I am glad to say, been infectious.

And, of course, last but not least, I owe everything to my family. To my grandparents, Mimi and Chimen, Mim and Bob, whose homes provided me with warmth, comfort, and a joyous sense of the power of good food and fine company when I was growing up. To my parents, Lenore and Jack Abramsky, who raised me to care and who taught me the power of love. To my brother, Kolya, and my sister, Tanya, who have always been there for me when I've wanted to laugh or needed to cry. To my wife, Julie Sze, an intellectual warrior in the best sense of the word, who has never yet encountered an idea she didn't want to know more about. Thank you for humoring me as I went down the sometimes dark road of reportage for this book. And to my two wonderful children, Sofia and Leo. You make our home come alive with joy and love, with curiosity and boundless chaos. You are the two most special little people in the world.

Note on Sources

Breadline USA is a work of journalistic reportage. The people quoted in this book are men, women, and children I met in person, talked with over the telephone, or corresponded with via email. In some cases I met with them multiple times; in others, just once. In many instances I followed up on my in-person meetings with phone calls during which we discussed particular themes growing out of our earlier encounters.

In any work of serious journalism, the anecdotes told by individuals, no matter how evocative they may be, are backed up by referencing broader research carried out by academic scholars, think tanks, government agencies, and nonprofit organizations. Journalists have many skills, but designing and implementing large-scale data-gathering projects are generally not among them. We are, after all, storytellers, first and foremost, rather than hunter-gatherers of primary data. Most often, journalists are content to rely on those of a more academic bent to generate the macro-data that back up their ideas. *Breadline USA* is no exception to this rule. Throughout its pages, I have quoted from Census Bureau, Department of Agriculture, and Labor Department data, as well as from reports commissioned by Second Harvest, the U.S. Conference of Mayors, the Food Resource and Action Center, and many other organizations. I have referenced large-scale studies by sociologists, political scientists, economists, and nutritionists.

Rather than clutter the text with footnotes, I have chosen to reference my sources in the narrative itself. In doing so, I trust that I have provided enough information that those looking for more in-depth sources will have little trouble finding the reports and studies upon which my work rests.

Prologue

This is the bread of poverty that our forefathers
ate in the land of Egypt. All who are hungry, let
them come and eat.

—Words from the Hagaddah, read at the Jewish Passover meal

WHEN I WAS A CHILD, GROWING UP in 1970s and 1980s London,
my grandparents' house was a magical place. My grandfather Chimen
was a history professor, my grandmother Mimi, a social worker. Their
home on the edge of Hampstead Heath—bought during the dog
days of World War II, when London was under aerial bombardment
and real estate could be had for a pittance—was an extraordinary
mixture of intellectual salon, place of refuge, and center of entertainment. People from around the world came to visit: family, friends,
friends of friends, strangers wanting good conversation and a hearty
meal. There were historians, artists, politicians, refugees, rabbis,
priests, musicians, exiles, orphans, and often just wandering travelers who'd heard about the legendary hospitality of my grandparents.
Nobody was turned away.

Whenever we showed up, someone was guaranteed to be staying in one of the spare bedrooms and someone else was frequently
camped out on a living room couch. When we went for meals, we
knew the attention of our grandparents would be shared among not
just us kids but numerous adults as well. Come Passover, the entire
house would become a food production site, with vegetable peel-

ers in one corner and kids putting smoked salmon on crackers in another; there'd be hard-boiled-egg shuckers, soup makers, turkey basters, and carvers.

Years later, after I moved to America and began hosting Thanksgiving dinners, my own house would acquire a similar aura that November day, one of uninhibited feasting and festivity. That sense of life-expressed-through-food is something I imbibed from birth, and it is something I will take with me throughout my life. Not just food-as-survival-material, but rather food-as-social-sustenance.

Mimi was a wonderful, if somewhat old-world, cook. There were always soups bubbling on the stove, chickens or ducks roasting in the oven, potato pancakes frying in hot oil, and, of course, extraordinary creamy dessert concoctions being carefully molded on the kitchen table. Mimi was a rather overweight diabetic with a sweet tooth, and when it came to sugar she lived vicariously through watching those she loved eat vast portions of the desserts she herself was no longer allowed (at least when others were watching) to indulge in. Her fridge was full of smoked salmon, borscht, orange juice, fruit, bowls of olives, sour cream, milk; in the freezer: kosher hotdogs, frozen milk popsicles, ice cream, vacuum-packed fillets of fish. In a little bread bin next to the freezer were loaves of sliced black rye bread and challah. Hidden away in cupboards were boxes of chocolates, wafer-biscuits, and KitKat chocolate bars.

For Mimi and Chimen, food was more than simply a meal; it was love, communication, a symbol of devotion and respect; it was a way to lubricate conversation and ward off loneliness and fear. Step into my grandparents' house, and you were stepping into a world of warmth in which to refuse food offered was to grievously disrespect your hosts. Mimi would sit you down, offer you food, ignore your protestations that you'd just eaten, trundle off into the kitchen, and return laden down with plates of goodies. If one of us didn't eat, her face would crease with concern borne out of love. *What's the matter? Are you sick? Don't you like my chicken? I can get you salmon? Soup?*

Maybe just some cake or chocolates? It was futile to resist; at some point during the visit, you were destined to encounter a plate of food.

Even today, I eat a bowl of matzo ball soup, or duck cooked a certain way, a few specimens of outlandishly creamy cakes, or smoked salmon on a particular kind of circular cracker, and I'm immediately transported back to my childhood, to the food-fugged warmth of my grandparents' kitchen. Neurologists believe these sorts of triggers fire up synapses that activate memories stored away years earlier, bringing them back to the surface of consciousness.

It is no accident that so many memories can be triggered by the smell and sight and texture of food. Throughout human history, the sharing of food, the breaking of bread with others, has been one of the signature themes for all major religions. We are hardwired to value the sharing of nutrition. Such sharing is a basic method by which the species survives. To share food is to share life. To let a person go hungry, to watch a fellow human being suffer so elementally, is to spit in the eye of God.

My grandmother was born in February 1917, the second of Bellafagel and Jacob Nierenstein's three daughters. She emerged into the desperate, grinding poverty of London's East End two and half years into what was already being called the Great War—the same East End that was churning out malnourished, stunted young men to serve as cannon fodder on the battlefields of France and Asia Minor (officers worried that their malnutrition would make them less effective warriors; hence were born bizarre high-energy culinary innovations such as the pungent-smelling yeast extract known as marmite). Mimi's parents owned a Jewish bookstore; they were part of the striving, hopeful generation of immigrants who left Russia and came to England and America in the early years of the twentieth century to make lives safe from pogroms and poverty. But while their dreams were large, their finances were small. Buying just the basics was a struggle; buying toys was a luxury. I remember my grandmother recollecting the joy she felt when, sometime in the early 1920s, she got one little doll to play with. Her smile, more than sixty years on, was the smile of a child reimagining a near-mythical extravagance.

The man Mimi ended up marrying, Chimen Abramsky, was born into the famine of Russia during World War I and grew into toddlerhood during the civil war that followed the Bolshevik Revolution. Family lore has it that this was the reason he only grew to five feet one inches tall. For those crucial first few years of life, Chimen didn't eat enough, didn't have enough milk to help him grow. Millions died of hunger in those years. The year my granddad and his family managed to leave the Soviet Union, 1932, Stalin created artificial food shortages in the Ukrainian countryside, and millions more lost their lives to empty bellies.

Mimi and Chimen's children, my father and my aunt, were born into an England devastated by another world war. My father was born during the blitz, in January 1942; his sister was born shortly after the war ended. During their childhoods England still suffered extreme food shortages, and most staples were heavily rationed. Even with money, there were strict limits on how much meat, butter, sugar, and chocolate one could buy. Nobody starved in England during this period, in marked contrast to continental Europe, where an extraordinary number of people died from hunger both during the war and in the desperately impoverished years following. But few ate with anything approaching abandon, either. Portions were meager; wasting food was considered an unspeakable act of social vandalism.

Now that I understand better the world that shaped my grandmother, I realize Mimi's compulsive overfeeding of her grandchildren was an entirely natural reaction to decades of deprivation. What she didn't have as a child, what she couldn't provide for her own children, she was determined, in more affluent times, to give her grandchildren. It irked us at the time. Sometimes, I'm ashamed to recall, I would shout at her and ask her to stop shoving food at me.

Now I know what she was doing—she was fattening us up for the lean times, pampering us while she could, doing everything in her power to make sure that the people nearest and dearest to her never went hungry. Now that I'm a father, I can only imagine how it must have hurt her to have her grandchildren shout at her when she tried to feed us.

A child who has been denied sufficient food, says Dr. Lynne Friedman-Gell, of the Susan B. Kravoy Eating Disorders Program, will likely experience long-term feelings of deprivation. "The child might then hide food away, because they're afraid they can't have it. Like a squirrel. They'll go into secret binges. They'll feel guilty about the binge, and if they worry about getting too heavy they'll throw up. It's the binge-purge cycle." More generally, hunger can lead to "anxiety issues, self-confidence, self-esteem issues. There's such a correlation of interrelatedness between all these different feelings. If you don't have enough food in your system it's hard to think. With children, cognitive development can be affected as well. It's hard to pay attention in school." Many psychologists believe that low self-esteem can, in turn, make a person more likely to turn to drugs or develop an alcohol dependency.

Parents might not generally know the ins and outs of deprivation theory. But they sure as hell know it's a bad thing to let their children go hungry. The urge to provide food to loved ones is as basic to our evolution as the sex urge, as much a part of who we are as the explorer impulse. We've inherited it from our primate ancestors, and they inherited it from their evolutionary predecessors. From the first moments chemicals linked themselves up into reproducible chains in the primordial ooze, the quest for sustenance has dominated animal behavior. Without this urge we couldn't exist. As the German philosopher Ludwig Feuerbach once wrote, man is what man eats. Take it to an extreme: you eat nothing, you *are* nothing.

Watch a bird carefully regurgitate food into the mouths of its young, and you're seeing a raw force of nature at work. Watch a human child devour handfuls of food, smearing the goo across her face, joyfully covering her body with edible detritus, and you're seeing uninhibited humanity in full Technicolor brilliance.

The week I started work on this book, I took my one-year-old son to the playground. In the little storage area under his stroller, I packed a loaf of bread. Leo, my son, toddled around the playground, made his way back to the stroller, grabbed at the loaf, and made grunting noises until I broke him off a chunk. He took it, held it protectively, raised it up to his face, and set his handful of teeth to work, madly masticating the doughy treat.

I felt insane pleasure. Those tiny, chubby hands grabbing the bread, that miniscule mouth greedily chewing the food, that potbelly under his T-shirt waiting to digest the mush: all were working in perfect harmony to convert food into energy, working to make my boy grow.

Not surprisingly, one critical measure used worldwide to determine if societies are developed, affluent, and successful is how well those societies can feed their own people: What is the average daily caloric intake of the population? When food prices rise, or crops fail, governments can tumble.

One of America's most remarkable traits over the centuries has been the abundance of food. Eighteenth- and nineteenth-century travelers marveled at the size of American portions. "All knives and forks were working away at a rate that was quite alarming," Charles Dickens wrote of his culinary experiences in the young United States. "Very few words were spoken; and everybody seemed to eat his utmost, in self defense, as if a famine were expected to set in before breakfast-time to-morrow morning." Aware of the staggering quantity of food consumed in his home country, Mark Twain observed, "A man accustomed to American food and American domestic cookery would not have starved to death suddenly in Europe, but I think he would gradually waste away and eventually die."

That excess of edibles, the almost carefree relationship most of America's population has to food, is something we take for granted; and yet, in human history it's something more than a rarity. America's food abundance and the global food gluts of the late twentieth and early twenty-first centuries are singularities, points of extraordinary departure from all previous human experience. Today, it's fashionable to scoff at Thomas Malthus's gloomy Enlightenment-era prognostications about the inevitability of famine as a curbing mechanism for human population growth. We look at industrial agriculture, modern medicine, and urbanization, and we see an earth that has absorbed vast population growth without, so far, collapsing into wholesale starvation. Yet rewind time just ever so slightly, and the world our great-grandparents were born into was, in many ways, a Malthusian one, with famines and epidemics routinely claiming the lives of millions.

Of course, beneath the surface, hunger in one form or another has always existed in America as well. Our narrative of plenty has never been universal. At one extreme there's the Donner Party story, that most famous of all heading-west-gone-wrong epics, when snow-stranded California pioneers in the winter of 1846–47 died atop the High Sierra and were eaten by their friends and relatives so that they might stay alive. More poetically, there are the numerous blues and folk songs detailing the gnawing daily hunger of America's working poor.

Read accounts of hardscrabble pioneer days on the farm; learn about the Dust Bowl, or Appalachian poverty; look at the photos of America's desperate poor taken by Walker Evans or Dorothea Lange, and in many ways you're reading and viewing a story we associate more with the Third World than with the United States of America. We know the hunger is out there in our history, but it doesn't tie in to the story we like to tell of ourselves. As a result, we generally banish it from view.

That feat of reimagining has been made easier by sixty-plus years of agricultural boom times, cheap food, and the existence of at least the rudiments of a social safety net. In the decades following World War II the country managed to minimize hunger, if not banish it. Programs such as Food Stamps, WIC (Special Supplemental Nutrition Program for Women, Infants, and Children), and welfare systems, such as Aid to Families with Dependent Children, provided some form of food and a financial safety net. At the same time farm productivity, riding a wave of scientific advances and access to cheap fertilizer, massively increased, leading to decades of food surpluses and generous U.S. Department of Agriculture donations to the country's emergent network of food banks. New Deal legacies such as Social Security and the minimum wage helped further squeeze hunger. Sure, hunger remained, but it was mainly the province of the homeless and the addicted, or people living in the most remote and underdeveloped rural regions. What it wasn't was a scourge for those with jobs and ambition, those who could be judged to be "playing by the rules" of the American Dream game. These were the years when, if anything, poor people got fat, their bodies soaking up the cheap, high-calorie, high-fat-and-sugar foods that came to dominate the aisles of most modern supermarkets.

Today, however, the economic equations underlying the Age of Affluence are breaking down, and a leaner, meaner version of hunger is once more stalking the land. A combination of global economic changes and domestic U.S. policies put in place from the 1980s through 2008 have come together to wreak havoc on the standard of living of ordinary Americans.

Globally, competition for natural resources in the early years of the century sharply pushed up the prices of energy, food, and raw materials. This price increase has had direct impacts—through far higher at-the-pump gas and diesel prices, higher heating bills, spiraling costs for groceries—and indirect ones, as service providers throughout the economy have had to find ways to cover the higher costs of manufacturing and transporting their wares. This part of the problem isn't unique to America. Reports out of England, France, Italy, Canada, and many other wealthy countries have, in recent years, documented a startling decline in the purchasing power of average citizens working average-paying jobs. Neither is the historically unprecedented rise in the cost of housing that occurred in the decade leading up to the 2007 housing bust entirely unique to the United States.

The second half of the equation, however, *is*, or at least *was* prior to the sea change ushered in by the 2008 presidential election result, made in the U.S. of A. It was formed by a series of conservative policy priorities—crafted over a generation—and economic calculi that, collectively, have served to catastrophically weaken the never particularly firm financial footing of America's poor.

Domestically, a series of changes in the way inflation is calculated has, in recent years, led government agencies to underestimate the erosion of consumers' purchasing power resulting from higher gas, food, health care, and housing prices, as well as to limit federal financial and food aid to people who meet an increasingly unreasonable definition of poverty. The federal poverty level for a family of four was, as of late 2008, $21,200 in the lower forty-eight states. For Hawaii and Alaska, it was slightly higher. For a single person it was a mere $10,590. Living-wage experts believe that the true level beneath which normal economic participation becomes impossible is over $22,000 for a single person. In the Californian coastal town of Santa Cruz, a living-wage ordinance takes that number as a threshold, mandating that workers employed by companies with public sector contracts be paid approximately eleven dollars per hour. At forty hours per week, that translates into $22,800 annually. A handful of other cities in the United States have adopted similar measures. The vast majority of Americans, however, do not live within living-wage zones. As a result of the outdated poverty-threshold criteria used by federal agencies, many millions of people, who by any stretch of the imagination are in dire financial straits, are deemed too affluent to qualify for Medicaid, food stamps, or even, for their kids, the school lunch program.

Making matters worse, access to welfare was also sharply curtailed by the 1996 welfare reforms, leaving large numbers of people cut off from financial aid; these reforms also placed lifetime limits on welfare program participation. In addition, the federal minimum wage stagnated from 1997 to 2007, its real purchasing power declining to levels not seen in a half century. A worker earning the $5.15 per hour minimum wage while working full time during these years would have brought in under eleven thousand dollars per year, just a couple hundred dollars above the official federal poverty level. Even with the raises to the minimum wage approved by Congress in 2007, hourly workers still only barely float above the poverty line.

Pushed off welfare, millions of Americans in the 1990s and 2000s ended up working for wages that didn't even begin to cover their basic everyday needs. Millions of others found service sector employment with companies like McDonald's and Wal-Mart, which, while paying higher than minimum wage, still paid far less than the amount needed to allow their employees to live halfway decent lives. As medical costs soared during these years, millions more—some working decently paid jobs—found themselves saddled with health-care debts and monthly premiums that devastated their family budgets.

These men and women live to work, unable to save money for a rainy day, borrowing off credit cards to pay bills and buy food they could not otherwise purchase, then borrowing off other credit cards—or, worse, high-interest payday loans—to service the original credit card debts that they can no longer keep ahead of. They perch atop tightropes, waiting for one ill wind to dash them to the ground.

Nationally, by mid-2008 nearly 28 million Americans were receiving food stamps—despite stringent eligibility restrictions and state application processes that frequently deterred the poor and hungry from seeking the aid. Over 30 million children were deemed poor enough to receive subsidized or free school lunches. More than 8 million women were accessing the WIC program for their infant children. And many millions of Americans were standing in line to take home the free bags of eatables provided by private donors and the U.S. Department of Agriculture (USDA) given out at food banks and pantries around the country. Untold millions more were scraping by without access to government aid—often their close-to-minimum-wage jobs pushed them over the qualification thresholds, despite the soaring costs of gas, heating, health care, and other necessities—and they were living too far away from food banks to have access to their charity.

In the cold bureaucratic language of the USDA, which studiously avoids using emotional terms such as "hunger," upward of 35 million Americans were "food insecure" by the end of the Bush presidency, which basically means they were expending a lot of energy to feed themselves and their families. Of these, more than 10 million had "very low food security," meaning they actually missed meals on a somewhat regular basis, skimped on their own portions so their kids could eat, and routinely ran into situations where they had no money to restock empty pantries.

By mid-2008, with unemployment and inflation both rising in near-lockstep, and with the home foreclosure crisis continuing apace, most experts agreed these numbers were going to get worse, were going to do so fairly quickly, and were going to stay bad for many years to come. The financial crisis that took down one major lending and investment institution after another in the summer and early autumn of 2008 made a bad problem even more dire, freezing up credit markets, at least temporarily collapsing stock values, and pushing already-on-the-edge companies into insolvency. Had the U.S. administration and the governments of other wealthy nations around the world not pumped trillions of dollars into rescuing the global financial system, much of the world could well have slipped into a long-term depression; as it is, even with the rescue packages in place, most experts believe the U.S. economy and others will face several years of serious financial recession.

Over the coming years, things probably won't get as bad as during the Great Depression, when up to one quarter of the U.S. workforce was unemployed and breadlines and shantytowns dotted every city; but that doesn't mean they won't still get pretty rough. As I write this prologue, we are in an after-the-fall moment. We know our economy has tumbled from a great height; we also know that the old, deregulation-based economic model suffered catastrophic organ failure. It created havoc in the financial, commercial, and eventually the manufacturing worlds; it resulted in extremes of economic inequality that ultimately brought poor and rich alike to the brink of ruin; and it ended up requiring emergency government intervention in the workings of the economy on an absolutely unprecedented scale. What we don't know yet—and likely won't know for several years—is exactly how bad the damage will be when things finally level out.

In part, the extent of the damage depends on the new institutions and the new social compact forged by Barack Obama's administration during its first years in office. President Obama was elected with a large enough mandate for fundamental change that he may well be able to create a twenty-first-century version of Roosevelt's New Deal, one that weaves a new social safety net for the next hundred years. If he does, if the nation's best and brightest are put to work designing public works programs, government-backed lending systems for businesses willing to invest in low-income communities, methods for keeping defaulting homeowners in their homes, an updated and expanded unemployment insurance plan, strong structures for guaranteeing retirement income, and a health-care system accessible by all, then, conceivably, the damage from the Bush years can be contained. But if Obama, for whatever reasons, cannot forge a fresh social compact and lock in place a new set of mutual obligations between state and populace, then the calamity of the 2008 economic collapse will haunt the next several decades of America's story.

President Obama himself assumed office with no illusion as to the gravity of the situation he was inheriting. "The road ahead will be long," he told his enthused supporters in Chicago's Grant Park on the night of his election victory. "Our climb will be steep. We may not get there in one year or even in one term. But, America, I have never been more hopeful than I am tonight that we will get there."

Like Franklin Delano Roosevelt three-quarters of a century before him, President Obama assumed power in a country beset by economic heartache. In the short term, at least, the new president's job will be as much about calming nerves as proposing solutions, holding fear in check while his administration works to put the country back on its feet once more. We know that in the short term, unemployment will continue to rise. That is an unavoidable legacy of the economic bust that provides an exclamation point to the Bush years. We don't know how long the recession will last or how low the stock market will go; how many companies, including industrial titans upon whom millions of workers and their families depend for a living, will bite the dust; how many families will have their life savings and their dreams destroyed. Nor do we yet know what government institutions will arise to ameliorate their pain. We don't know how many millions will find the search for work so disillusioning that they eventually drop out of the workforce. Nor can we fully predict the social ramifications of dried-up credit combined with the wholesale economic collapse of entire communities. But we can predict that, even with a newly interventionist mood in Washington, D.C., even with a new administration passionately committed to notions of social justice and economic dignity for ordinary workers, for many Americans the coming years will be strikingly hard; the legacy of decades of deregulation and "trickle-down" economics will mean poverty and an increased inability to provide even the basics—including adequate food—for themselves and their families.

According to the international food expert Christopher Dunford, director of the California-based group Freedom From Hunger, these people already experience a "chronic hunger," or at least the fear of going hungry, comparable to that experienced by workers in developing countries, "anxieties caused by the perception you're not going to have enough food; the anxiety of not being able to accomplish the minimum responsibility you have to you and your family." That doesn't mean they're starving. What it means is that like many of the 1 billion chronically hungry people worldwide, they're not getting enough to eat or enough varieties of food to constitute a healthy, balanced diet. The acquisition of food has, for them, become a consuming quest. Ongoing low-level hunger can, Dunford says, impair the cognitive development of children, reduce their school achievement, lower the functionality of adults, decrease economic productivity, and compromise individuals' immune systems. "This kind of anxiety is debilitating," he explains.

Dunford argues that the loss of a job or a cut in hours for an on-the-edge American worker can have the same catastrophic impact as local crop failures in a developing nation or the loss to disease of a peasant farmer's livestock. "Do people have a stream of resources that enables them to get enough food? And if that stream gets interrupted, do they have enough assets to have people to turn to? Truly poor people don't have people to turn to. They have very little social capital. In a place like India, there's enough food to feed every Indian. Access is the issue, the extreme differences in people's ability to pay for food or grow their own food. The same in America. That's really what poverty's all about no matter where you are."

As a result, for millions of Americans today the real "omnivore's dilemma," to use Michael Pollan's term from his book of that title, is not *what* to eat, but *whether* to eat. What do you do when you have to choose between paying the rent or mortgage and going to the supermarket; between filling your car with gas to drive to work and adequately feeding your children; between buying necessary medications or paying for necessary medical care and going to bed with a full stomach? What do you do when you work as hard as you can, live frugally, and still end up with an empty wallet and an empty fridge a week before your next paycheck?

After years of inactivity in the face of America's growing hunger crisis, the ability to create solutions to these dilemmas should be a key litmus test for measuring the success or failure of the new administration in D.C.

President Barack Obama's election was an astounding, transformative moment. Tens of millions of voters, from the most liberal to the most conservative regions of the country, stood up and said "no more" to the divisive, greed-driven policies and priorities of the recent past. That act opens up a once-in-a-generation possibility for reinventing and reinvigorating the American Dream. For those who have lost out during the casino-capitalism experiment started by Ronald Reagan and ignominiously concluded under George W. Bush nearly three decades later, there is at least the hope that life will start to change for the better. If it does, then the new administration will have already started to secure its long-term legacy.

Breadline USA is, as the title implies, a story of American hunger. In researching this book, I interviewed numerous people around the country about their experiences. At a certain point, though, I realized that was not enough. I had been thinking about dipping my feet into the waters of food insecurity; then, in a hotel room in Siskiyou County, California, I watched Gregory Peck in the movie *Gentleman's Agreement*. The journalist Peck portrayed was writing on anti-Semitism. Wrestling with how to tell the story, he realized he could never get the whole picture unless he experienced it himself; and, so, for the duration of his research, he played himself off as a Jew. The film sealed the deal. Two days later, I began a series of low-income food experiments.

Unlike the thirty-six conscientious objectors who volunteered to be part of a starvation experiment run by nutritionist Ancel Keys at the University of Minnesota in Minneapolis in 1944–45 and designed to work out how to most effectively build back up a body emaciated by starvation, the point of my work, despite my four-year-old daughter's overwrought concern, was *not* to starve myself. I have neither the desire, nor, I fear, the self-control, to put myself through such an ordeal. In his massive book on the experiment, *Biology of Human Starvation*, Keys wrote of the disappearance of nearly all body fat during periods of prolonged starvation; the swelling of soft tissue due to water retention; muscular atrophy; a shrinkage in the size of many important body organs—including the liver and kidneys, though not the brain, which seems remarkably resilient to weight loss; and a startling slowdown of the pulse rate. Even small glands, like the thyroid, began to atrophy. The hair of many of his volunteers began to fall out, their bones started to weaken—although not to the extent seen in victims of even more extreme food deprivation—their skin became pallid and scaly, and their sex drives disappeared. After months of appalling hunger, even the most socially engaged of his volunteers could think, and dream, of nothing but food.

Hunger, wrote Harvard physiologist Walter B. Cannon, in his classic 1929 text *Bodily Changes in Pain, Hunger, Fear and Rage*, "is a sensation so peremptory, so disagreeable, so tormenting, that men have committed crimes in order to assuage it. It has led to cannibalism, even among the civilized. It has resulted in suicide. And it has defeated armies."

Recreating the Minnesota project was not what I wanted to do. Rather, my aim was to see how low-income Americans *avoided* going hungry; and how that avoidance has, in recent years, become increasingly difficult. Like the people I interviewed, I wanted to create financial conditions, based around economic realities described to me by people on the front lines of hunger, that would make me *worry* about food, that would force me to stop taking its availability for granted, and that would make me calculate my expenditures, and my food consumption, down to the penny and the individual meal.

When I was in college, I routinely went hungry, or, at the very least, sated my hunger with the sorts of cheap, greasy, filling food my body now rebels against. There was nothing remotely unique about this. Most of my friends, and probably many of my readers, slummed it to one extent or another while cramming for their degrees. And if we didn't go hungry in college, we probably have gone hungry at other times, perhaps listened as our bellies growled during camping trips while the fires wouldn't light or when we misjudged the amount of food to bring along. There's a sense of adventure, camaraderie, or youthful derring-do to these experiences. What there isn't is a sense of grinding permanence. We know the camping trip will soon be over, and we'll get back to our creature comforts; we know we'll all too soon be facing our graduation moment, heading out into the wide world, and landing lucrative, professional jobs. Our days of hunger are playful, badges of honor in an affluent culture. What most of us don't know is the sort of ongoing hunger, the desperate nervousness about food and cash that shuts down your horizons, limits your social circles, embarrasses you into invisibility, shames you when you venture out in public. Yet that is the sort of boundless hunger, the unpleasant fear that tens of millions of working Americans today face on a daily basis. And that is what I felt I had to know to write this book.

A few years back, the self-proclaimed "money guru" David Bach came up with the idea of a Latte Factor. It was the amount of money middle-class Americans would casually throw away on caffeine drinks, pastries, glasses of wine, and other nutritional and stimulus-based fripperies quite separate from their basic, necessary grocery bills. The idea caught on, and if you go online today, you'll find numerous Latte Factor Web sites, even calculators that allow you to work out your personal Latte Factor and how much you could save or earn by investing that money elsewhere. In 2005, a *USA Today* journalist estimated that a New Yorker who was spending seven dollars a day on a pack of cigarettes could earn $3.6 million over fifty years by investing that money instead and reaping a 10 percent annual return. That's a lot of cash.

I'd never thought that much about it, but when I started doing the numbers my Latte Factor was huge: a coffee and a chocolate bis-cotti at my local café during my once-a-day break from working in the office I've carved out of a room in my house. Right there, with tip, that's four dollars a day. Then there's the odd days when I splurge and get two coffees, or a cappuccino instead of a coffee—an increas-ing rarity these days, with utility bills rising and double day-care costs. Then there are a couple visits a week to the pub, snacks from snack machines when I teach late at night, bottles of water or soda to cool me down while I'm exercising, needless lunches at cafés, not because I'm meeting a friend but because I'm too lazy to cook. My modest Latte Factor? Somewhere between sixty and one hundred dollars each week. Far more than a member of the new working poor can spend on all their food needs in a two-week pay period.

To really understand what these people were going through, what emotions were running through their heads, what they dreamt about on empty stomachs, I needed not just to intellectually empathize with them, but, more viscerally, to experience their hunger pangs. For seven weeks during the research for this book I put myself in their shoes. I estimated what a low-income employee would earn every two weeks; I had my accountant work out what the tax obliga-tions would be on that; I talked with low-income workers to find out how much they tended to spend on rent, car payments, gas, utilities, servicing credit card debt, and health-care needs; and I extrapolated how much I would realistically have left to spend on food during a two-week pay cycle.

The first thing to go was my Latte Factor. No more trips around the corner to Freeport Bakery to grab those precious few minutes of communal time during days spent working alone at home; no more quick lunches on the backyard patio of Dads' Kitchen; no more four-dollar burritos from the local Salvadoran hole-in-the-wall, or seven-dollar burgers at ten o'clock Monday evenings after teaching my university writing class, or weekend brunches with my wife and kids. Unless my drinking buddies were buying, no weekly visits to the English pub in downtown Sacramento for a couple pints with some of my local writing friends. And certainly no more treks to the extravagantly well-stocked, but rather overpriced, local deli-cum-butcher's. The sorts of fresh meat and fish I normally buy there were now as far outside my culinary range as caviar is to me in my everyday middle-class life.

I didn't want the rest of my family to go hungry, so I carved out for myself a shelf in the fridge and one kitchen cupboard. Next to my family's eatables—that, as the weeks went by, looked increasingly like little offerings of paradise—I stacked my pathetic ingredients.

For nearly two months, I set myself six different permutations on poverty, each of them modeled on stories and situations told to me by the working poor around America, and every week or two I mildly tweaked the conditions of my poverty. For the first couple weeks I assumed I was working as many hours as I could, that my credit cards were still good (allowing me to go modestly over budget if need be) and that I had access—as I do, in fact, have—to an extremely affordable farmers market for fruits and vegetables. Gradually, I tightened my conditions. My gas expenses increased by ten dollars a week (as they did for average drivers in the first months of 2008). My hours were cut. I endured an unexpected but unavoidable extra expense that threw my weekly financial calculations off. My proximity to the farmers market and to quality supermarkets was eradicated and replaced by access only to an overpriced corner store in a poor part of town; at this store I limited myself to spending the twenty-six dollars I would get in food stamps each week as an average single, impoverished person. Since most people below the federal poverty line do not have credit cards, I did not give myself this option for additional spending. And, finally, I removed my eligibility for food stamps and returned to my low-income employment budget without even the twenty-six-dollar food stamp safety net to fall into.

The intent was to fill in the reporting gap—to get a sense of what it feels like to go to bed on an empty belly, to stand in line at a food pantry, to lug a box of charity food home two miles when money to buy gas for the car has run out. I didn't refuse invitations to people's houses, or turn down free cakes at university office parties—after all, I wasn't trying to go hungry; nor, though, did I go out of my way to score invitations or find free cake.

While this is mainly a book about other people, in part it is about my experiences, too. The weeks I tried to live within extremely limited food budgets were some of the hardest weeks of my life—not because I literally starved but because I was in a continual state of anxiety, because food and how to procure it rapidly became the central focal point of my waking hours. And if that's the case for someone only doing an experiment, someone with money in the bank, with a full pantry to fall back on if need be, with options and choices and the knowledge that everything would revert to normal in a few weeks, and with none of the accompanying symptoms of modern poverty—lack of health-care access, anxiety about home foreclosure, kids left unattended because the parents are working multiple jobs, and so on—I can only imagine how much worse are the food anxieties of the truly poor.

My experiences show up as short interludes between the main chapters of this book. Their intent is not to grandstand but rather to fill in the gaps left when I, the reporter, had to leave my sources alone to navigate their emotions and fears and middle-of-the-night anxieties.

ONE

—

Driving to Hunger

The one who rides knows not the trials
of walking; he who is full does not know
the bitterness of hunger.

—ANONYMOUS, Chinese proverb

FORT JONES, CALIFORNIA, is a classic Old West town, with the
paint peeling off its antiquated wooden buildings and a Main
Street that, in physical appearance, hasn't changed much in a century. There's an old hardware store, brick bank buildings, a couple
Mexican restaurants, and a smattering of saloons. The few hundred
residents mostly live in mobile homes or small wooden houses that
look like they have been sitting there forever yet seem utterly fragile,
as if it would take only one abnormally strong gust of wind to blow
them into oblivion. Other communities in the region have a similar aura about them. Hamlets such as Dunsmuir, Weed, Callahan,
and the larger town of Yreka. Yreka—one of the few urban hubs in
Siskiyou County and the neighboring area not to have witnessed a
population decline since 1990—still calls itself "The Golden City,"
an optimistic throwback to its glory days, and still boasts Wild West
saloons and elegant Victorian edifices along its central drags, Main
and Miners streets. Similarly, the little railway town of Dunsmuir
prides itself on its charming, somehow anachronistic eccentricity;
in the window of a downtown law office is a plaster-cast skeleton
reclining in a dentist's chair, an aviator's leather cap and goggles

adorning its skull. Like moth-worn cashmere sweaters, these towns provide glimpses of past, unrecoverable grandeur.

Fort Jones feels old and crotchety, yet feisty, still echoing with memories of the Gold Rush that hit California's mountainous far north over a century and half ago. Residents have gone through good times and bad over the years. These days, however, they're stuck firmly in the bad times, and all indications are those times will only be getting worse.

Sandwiched in between an old fire station and an oversized wooden barn, on a dusty little side street off the main road, is a small food pantry run by volunteers from a local church. In this building, as in so many others like it across the country, day by day an American Tragedy is exposed; at the same time, a heroic community response is enacted. To the pantry come the community's hungry and desperate—not hoboes and vagrants who have spent years off the grid, but the new working poor, men and women who have played by the rules their whole lives, but who, in early-twenty-first-century America, can no longer make it on their own. To the pantry, too, come people who donate food, volunteers who collect food from food banks, restaurants, and supermarkets, and more volunteers to distribute that food to their neighbors in need.

Like the town they live in, George and Billy MacPherson are getting on in years—they were both born in the late 1920s—but they also remain joyfully feisty. Billy dresses in jeans and a flowery blouse, a small gold cross dangling from her neck; George is in old, stained jeans and a short-sleeved shirt, red suspenders crossed in the back, a leather patch reading "Grizzly," a baseball cap, and weathered brown cowboy boots. A friendly smile lurks under his gray moustache. Other than the plastic wristwatch on his left wrist, George presents the image of a farmer from pre–World War II days. George's father brought him north to Siskiyou from Los Angeles when he was a toddler to work a gold mine stake; at sixteen, Billy moved west with her parents—both of them country schoolteachers—from Oilton, Oklahoma, during World War II. The couple met when they were both in high school, at a bowling alley where Billy's older sister ran a sandwich concession, and they got married the week Billy turned eighteen. As the war drew to a close, George was drafted; he served in the military until 1947.

In the years after the Allied victory, as George tried his hand at various careers and four children were born in quick succession, the MacPherson family, like many of their rural neighbors, had no money. "When our kids were growing up, we scrounged food any place we could," George recalled. "A lot of the old orchards. We weren't the kind of people to sit around and starve. We scrounged food from the old homesteads. There'd be a lot of fruit trees. We raised our kids on venison. In those days, it didn't really matter; there were so many deer. But when they put the freeway in and the roads started killing the deer off, we didn't have as many deer. In the Depression, a lot of people existed because they had venison." (In Nevada, I once met a man in his sixties who recalled that the only meat he ever ate as a child was from squirrels that he and his father used to shoot. The family simply couldn't afford to buy meat. That experience, he explained, was why he would never support a political candidate who proposed limitations on gun ownership.) Billy remembered how they often went weeks on end eating only pancakes. "We'd get down to where we had pancakes and butter and syrup. And before we got any money we'd be down to pancakes *without* butter and syrup." The flour and water mix might not be nutritious, but it was cheap and would temporarily stop a stomach from rumbling.

Memories like that don't die easily. Perhaps that's why, more than a half century later, the couple looked around their community, saw a tremendous number of their neighbors going hungry again, and decided to work through their church to found a little food pantry in Fort Jones.

"Hunger hurts. It hurts to be hungry," Billy said simply, in explanation. "Times are getting really tight." Many of their clients were so broke they couldn't even afford cooking oil to fry up the food donations from the pantry, so the volunteers started filling old salad-dressing bottles with corn oil and distributing them to the hungry. Billy's husband chipped in, talking of the increasing number of hungry people and the falloff in food contributions to the pantry as the economy worsened. "The harder times become, the scarcer food becomes. We don't have the donations. It's when we need the food the most that we get the least."

Children came into the pantry and jumped for joy when Billy and George gave them coloring pencils or cupcakes. "They don't have anything," George said. "Anything you gave them, they were so emotional about it." One old lady began crying when the pantry workers gave her a couple rolls of toilet paper—it was a luxury she'd had to forgo in recent years as her Social Security checks got eaten away by inflation.

Over the months I worked on this book, I encountered similar stories all over the country, stories of older men and women spending almost all their money driving to visit their doctors in the cities, retreating back to their homesteads afterward, and coming to town only to pick up food, kitchen supplies, and toiletries at pantries. For food charity workers in states like Oklahoma, the remoter corners of their states were no longer the romantic, harsh-but-pure idylls of Laura Ingalls Wilder's writings; instead they were "food deserts," places whose residents were under siege by high energy costs and a lack of ready access to affordable food.

English and American trappers from the 1820s onward explored the mountains and rivers of the Siskiyou region. With the discovery of gold in northern California in the late 1840s, the area's population soared. For a time after the precious metal was found in the gold camp of Yreka in 1849, the improvised town became known as "the richest square mile on earth."

The boom times didn't last. By the early 1850s, local residents were complaining that the region was being ignored by the rest of the new state. It was, they bemoaned, a place known for its mines and its logging industry, its stunning scenery, and its remoteness, but not a place the state was investing much energy in developing. They became so angry that in the early 1850s residents of Siskiyou County and neighboring communities in northern California and the southern Oregon region attempted to form their own state, Jefferson. The effort failed, but the grievances remained. Over the decades, Siskiyou increasingly lagged behind the rest of California in economic development. In the first decade of the twenty-first century, with the decline of the local logging industry, Siskiyou County was becoming ever more impoverished. Unemployment grew, up to nearly 10 percent by 2006, at a time when the statewide average was below 5 percent. More damaging, however, was that the jobs that *did* exist were increasingly low-wage service sector jobs. Many of the young people were leaving, and the average age of the population was rising. In 1990, the county had close to 7,000 residents in the thirty- to thirty-nine-year-old age bracket. By the early years of the following decade, that number was down to 3,500. Conversely, the number of residents in the fifty- to fifty-nine-year-old bracket had risen from about 4,300 to almost 7,500. That meant a lower tax base and more need for services.

What Siskiyou County and numerous other remote regions around the United States are experiencing is the American Dream in reverse, a story of diminishing possibilities and increasing obstacles to success, a saga of exodus rather than influx.

At the same time, the tech boom was making large numbers of Silicon Valley residents overnight millionaires, and they began buying second homes up near Mount Shasta. Log cabins in the town of Mt.

Shasta itself were selling for as much as $1 million before the housing bubble burst, pushing prices up and forcing hardscrabble locals further out onto the economic margins. Twenty years before, a house in one of these towns would have sold for about $40,000; by the early 1990s, it had increased to $60,000; and in 2008, even after the bursting of the housing bubble, those same houses were selling for over $250,000. Because many local jobs pay at, or just above, the minimum wage, many residents were forced to spend almost all their income on housing, leaving little for other necessities, including food. These are the folks, asserted Pinky Hines, organizer of the Dunsmuir Food Pantry, who come to her for help. "At least twenty-five percent or more [of the local population] are in sad shape," Pinky estimated. "Most of the people needing food help are the young, working poor, who're stretched beyond [the] breaking point by inflated housing prices."

Bureau of Economic Analysis (BEA) data indicated that Siskiyou County's per capita personal income (an aggregate number that includes earnings and various other income generators) was $23,226 in the middle years of the first decade of the new century, only 76 percent of the national average and ranking it forty-five out of fifty-eight among California counties. Subtract the government jobs in the county seat of Yreka, and the numbers were even worse: the unincorporated town of McCloud, for example, had a per capita income of slightly under $16,000. Those sorts of numbers add a whole new level of intensity to the word "hardscrabble."

Whatever employment there is in Siskiyou County is concentrated in a handful of towns: there's a Wal-Mart on the southern edge of Yreka; the county has a water bottling plant that packages glacial waters from Mount Shasta; there are the usual cookie-cutter malls in Redding, to the south; and there are the hotels and restaurants that cater to tourists. "We don't have very much work in the community right now," Mike Stacher, general manager of the McCloud Community Services District, said. "We have eight-dollar-an-hour jobs here, which is unlivable as far as I'm concerned."

Siskiyou County is almost as large as New Jersey but has a population of only about 45,000. More than one hundred miles north of California's capital city, Sacramento, the endless farmlands of the Central Valley give way to forested mountains and breathtaking grasslands. It is a remote landscape—more akin to Wyoming's Big Sky country than to the rest of California—one dominated by the fourteen-thousand-feet-high glacier-covered Mount Shasta and the menacing clouds that frequently cluster around its peak. New Agers believe Shasta has a sacred aura. Setting aside the fuzzy imagery, it's certainly a remarkable presence. On a clear day, you can see its jagged slopes from well over one hundred miles away. Distance, and thus reliance on one's car to get between the far-flung towns and villages, is an irreducible fact of daily life. As a result, the region's population is particularly vulnerable to oil price fluctuations, particularly at risk of economic catastrophe when at-the-pump gas prices soar, as they did throughout much of the first decade of the century. As oil prices began an upward march that would ultimately, at least temporarily, quadruple at-the-pump prices, Siskiyou County's residents faced a succession of body blows to the kidneys. Off the public transport grid and the major oil distribution network, the area suffered through a period of fuel costs that were even higher than elsewhere. Gas and diesel ran about fifteen cents a gallon higher than the statewide average; at least as damaging, propane and kerosene, used by many residents to heat their houses during the brutal alpine winters, became prohibitively expensive. Gas hit three dollars a gallon in Siskiyou County shortly after Hurricane Katrina, in 2005, shut down Gulf Coast pipelines and oil wells for several weeks. It hit four dollars a gallon in early April 2008. By June 2008, it was heading toward five dollar territory.

What does all this mean? A perfect storm of economic changes risks rendering the towns of this region, places like McCloud and Yreka, unlivable for working-class residents, administering a coup de grâce to a region already bedeviled by blue-collar job loss and a corresponding decline in the working-age population. In the same way that the end of ready pickings from the gold fields created depopulated mining towns—ghost towns—throughout much of the West, so the series of ascending oil price spikes from 2005 through 2008 began to profoundly alter the Western landscape, as well as many other remote, car-dependent regions of the country. In the Santa Fe Trail town of Boise City, Oklahoma, a place that not too long ago boasted a thriving little downtown, residents openly talked of the city becoming a ghost town. Young people were fleeing, and not far shy of half the remaining residents survived on handouts from the local food pantry. In the agricultural community of Melrose, New Mexico, a similarly grim story held: One store after another on Main Street had closed in recent years, local farmers had hit bottom as fuel and fertilizer costs rose, and the aging population, stranded a half hour's drive from the nearest supermarkets, was living off Social Security checks and trucked-in charity food.

On June 9, 2008, the *New York Times* published a county-by-county map showing what percentage of their income residents were, on average, spending on gas. Wilcox County, in southern Alabama, came in first, at 16 percent; Holmes County, in central Mississippi, wasn't far behind, at 15.6 percent. In the same general ballpark were a number of counties in Arkansas, the Dakotas, Indiana, Kentucky, Oklahoma, Tennessee, Texas, and Wyoming.

Fifty-one-year-old Neal Owen was one of those hit particularly hard by rising energy prices. Fifteen years earlier, Owen had seriously injured his back while working as a slab man for a trucking outfit. A tire he was working on exploded and hit his back with tremendous force. He soldiered on for a decade, but in his mid-forties he had to quit work and go on disability. His wife still worked full time at a local factory, but her small salary, which netted her around $1,300 per month, together with his $750 disability payment, no longer covered all their bills.

Owen was a rugged-looking man in jeans, a white T-shirt, suede shoes, and a baseball cap, his hair pulled back in a long ponytail, his face covered by a thick, graying beard. The couple lived out in Greenview, a small enclave several miles from Fort Jones, into which Owen had to drive regularly to see his doctor.

In 2006, Neal bought a twelve-year-old pickup truck, which he hoped would navigate the tough winter terrain as well as provide enough space for their three young granddaughters, who were living with them at the time. It came with 100,000 miles on it and, on a good day, did fifteen miles to the gallon. They kept their other car, an '88 Ford Mustang, but it needed repairs, and as they couldn't afford the extra expense, the car sat idle on their property.

As gas and heating costs escalated, the family fell further and further behind. In 2004, the Owens had installed a propane heating system on their property. In winter, they'd go through a one-hundred-gallon tank every two weeks; at the time, with propane at $1.20 a gallon, it wasn't a big deal. By 2008, however, it was costing $330 to fill their tank, and they were spending nearly $700 a month in winter just to heat their home. As 2009 approached, the couple decided to disconnect the propane system and instead start scavenging wood to burn in an old-fashioned furnace. Neal, who had recently enrolled at the College of the Siskiyous, at Weed, to study for an associate's degree in computer science, was spending another $80 to $100 a week on gas for his truck. Factor in monthly payments on the Owens' credit card debt, prescription costs, and all the other little bills, and the couple was stretched beyond the breaking point. With expenses far outstripping income, Neal was thinking about dropping out of college—a decision he knew would mean he'd almost certainly never work again.

"It's getting to be kind of a drag," Neal said, as he stocked up on food from the pantry. "My wife's working full time and all, and we still don't have money to do anything. The cupboards are bare, and there's no money. We come [to the pantry] when there's no money.

This'll help us through to my wife's next payday. I can't even afford the gas to go fishing, and that's my main enjoyment."

Siskiyou's residents were learning an uncomfortable truth. Whether or not the earth has reached a "peak oil" point—at which global producers can't increase daily supplies of oil to meet escalating demand—supply over the past decade has gotten tight and will likely get tighter in the years ahead. This trend is an inevitable byproduct of globalization, of an increasingly integrated world economy. It is, if you like, a side effect of shared prosperity.

OPEC and the world's other large producers can probably keep pumping enough oil for the next several decades to allow several hundred million people to consume large quantities of oil without worrying too much about its impact on their finances. In the past, those several hundred million were largely concentrated in a handful of countries in North America, Western Europe, Australasia, and Japan. For generations of Americans, in particular, car ownership and high gas consumption were considered almost birthrights. Now, in a global era, affluent elites worldwide—in China, India, Mexico, Egypt—are also clamoring for oil. In response, the immutable laws of supply and demand are, over the long term, pushing energy prices up. This increase in price, in turn, makes trading in oil more tempting for speculators, thus further contributing to the increasing price volatility in the commodities markets in the first decade of the twenty-first century.

In short, while America's elites will not face gas shortages or truly unaffordable prices anytime soon, working families are increasingly finding that fuel consumption is no longer something to be taken for granted. As in so many other countries, transport had become a major financial headache for tens of millions of low-income Americans.

"I'm spending forty to fifty dollars a week on gas," forty-one-year-old Rosie Kerr, a resident of Grenada, California, told me two weeks after Hurricane Katrina. She was working, at the time, as a secretary at the Northern California Indian Development building on Yreka's Main Street and was driving a 1992 blue Ford Explorer with 162,000 miles on it.

After taxes and health insurance deductions, Kerr, a mother of four, whose husband was unemployed at the time, estimated that she took home about $1,200 per month. The higher gas prices had forced her to borrow from her mother just to be able to continue working. "My mother helps me. That's the only way I've been making it back and forth for the past few months. I owe my mom thousands of dollars for gas. It doesn't feel very good. It literally makes me feel like a heel. Because I can't pay her back. And she's been helping me with food, too, because I don't have enough income for that either."

Twenty miles east of the interstate stopping point of Dunsmuir, thirty-seven-year-old McCloud resident Christine Gannon estimated that she and her husband were spending three hundred dollars a month on gas for their vehicles and another few hundred on oil for the generators that supplied electricity to their mountainside house. Like Christine, many of Siskiyou County's residents live in remote locales, where they have little choice but to drive gas-guzzling pickup trucks that can navigate back roads in winter and agricultural terrain year-round. The terrain and the architecture of the place pretty much require such vehicles.

Christine had recently moved from a job at a hardware store that paid $7.25 an hour to an AmeriCorps position with the McCloud Resource Center that paid only marginally more. Her husband, a truck driver for a fuel delivery company, had an income that fluctuated monthly. The family had health insurance, but it came with a hefty four-thousand-dollar annual deductible. They had student loans to pay off, car payments to make, and two growing boys to feed. Add in the extra few thousand dollars a year they were spending on gas, compared to just a year or two earlier, and something had to give.

"We've had to cut back on entertainment. We've had to cut back on filling the house with groceries and having plenty of snackables," Christine said. "No vacations. We've had to postpone putting money away to buy a home. It makes me feel like having a decent home and decent life without having to stress constantly and worry, it seems like it's just never going to happen; and dreams and hope and plans, they just don't work out."

Amy Detrick, a secretary in the county administration office, had started taking the bus instead of driving to work from the tiny village of Etna. Her daughter, however, didn't have that option. She worked at a Subway shop in Yreka, a job that netted her about three hundred dollars per week. She got off work at nine thirty in the evening, after the busses stopped running; she had no choice but to drive the more than thirty miles each way to and from work. Even in her new Honda Civic, bought with help from her parents, that was close to ten dollars a day in gasoline costs, or almost 20 percent of her income.

"What are you going to do? Not work?" asked Mike Stacher. "Maybe it'll get to a point where not working is an option."

For Rosie Kerr's two brothers, that point had already been reached. A month before I met Rosie, as gasoline prices began hitting record highs, the two men had both quit their jobs in McCloud. They could no longer afford to drive their pickup trucks the fifty-plus miles each way from their homes in Hornbrook, a small community several miles north of Yreka. It was, quite literally, more financially sensible to become unemployed and join the legion of casual workers picking up local bit-work whenever possible.

On the Navajo Reservation in western New Mexico, a similarly grim equation was in play. Many people on the reservation live on family land, handed down over the generations; the land is sere—a desert wilderness of red-rock canyons and mesas, marginally farmable in good years, viciously arid during droughts. Half the houses out on the reservation still lack running water and electricity. For employment, many drive their pickup trucks scores of miles to

Gallup, a small town just east of the Arizona border, to work in jew-elry and pottery stores, construction, or government jobs; or they go to other, smaller towns such as Cuba. "It's pretty far to come from where I live to town," said one twenty-nine-year-old woman who had driven from her home in White Horse to the food pantry in Gallup. "We only get to come into town once in every great while. It's like twenty dollars, thirty dollars in gas. I only come in if I have to. I had to make an appointment with food stamps, but in the meantime I ran out of food. I feed my three boys potatoes. Just potatoes and tortillas. When there was a ceremony going they gave us the leg of a sheep and that's what we've been eating. It lasted two weeks. We eat two meals a day. Just breakfast and dinner. Usually oatmeal for breakfast and in the evening gravy potatoes with tortillas." Before gas prices got so high, the young lady had worked in a 7-Eleven store in Cuba, earning $6.80 an hour and working about forty hours a week. "Then gas prices went so high. All at one time it went through the roof." Spending close to half her income on gasoline to drive to work made no sense, so she quit her job and the family joined America's new hungry poor.

"At this moment, at home, I have potatoes, flour, dried milk. Prob-ably six potatoes left. And a mutton neck. That's it. And Kool-Aid. But we don't have no more sugar. All my sons drink is dried milk."

These are people who count pennies in the best of times, who are continually juggling rent and food and medical bills, who tap their resources days before the start of a new pay cycle and routinely resort to credit card debt and other borrowing to weather the lean times. Earning little and already spending a disproportionate amount of their income on gasoline, people like Rosie Kerr were, in the years following 2005, being subjected to an inflationary spiral, one un-noticed by the media and most politicians, far in excess of that expe-rienced by consumers who were only spending 3 to 5 percent of their income on gasoline. Moreover, in regions such as Siskiyou County, where everything has to be delivered long distances, as gas prices soared, so, too, did the cost of other goods.

"Where I used to deliver free all of my printing jobs, I can no longer do so," explained fifty-nine-year-old Lyle Sauget, owner of a Yreka print shop. "If it's local, I charge one dollar. If it's Mt. Shasta or Weed, it's five to seven dollars. My printing prices are cheaper. But when you factor in fuel prices, I could be pricing myself out of the market. Fuel is affecting everything. Food. Clothing. Everything's gone up. When they [locals] are already on a tight budget, it makes it pretty difficult. It takes an already depressed area and takes it down. As a business person, at a certain point you say 'I'd rather go work for someone out of the area than be a business owner.'"

When gas hit three dollars a gallon, Kerr began changing her own oil and tried, as best she could from reading a few car maintenance books, to give her Explorer its needed tune-ups. "I can't afford to go downtown to have someone else do it for me," she explained. "I've thought about selling some of my stuff. I have some antique radios from my grandmother. I've been putting that off for a year now. I can't fill my tank. I haven't been able to fill my tank in a year or two. I do twenty dollars here, twenty there. I do without food to get gas, pretty much regularly. There's never any breakfast. Nobody eats breakfast in my house. My mom feeds me lunch after she gets off work. Maybe two times a week we go without dinner. Eat nothing. My boss was nice enough to let me cash in some vacation time last month, so I had enough to buy some groceries."

As long as people live in regions like Siskiyou County and commute to jobs far away in places that are hard, if not impossible, to reach via public transport, they are going to need gas; and as long as they need gas simply to continue working, they are going to do whatever it takes—shortchanging themselves on food and medicine; putting the gas on credit cards and hoping, somehow, to pay it off down the road; deferring needed repairs on their cars or hoped-for upgrades to better, more fuel-efficient vehicles—to keep their vehicles running. After all, entire communities, lifestyles, job choices, and consumption patterns have been crafted, over the better part of a century, around the notion of cheap and plentiful gas supplies. Suddenly change the equation without offering any government relief or large-scale strategic planning, and, even though gas remains cheaper per gallon than in much of the rest of the world, the relative difference proves disastrous. Unless there is some government intervention, people will have no choice but to desperately try to absorb the higher costs. Such intervention could come in the form of subsidies designed to encourage people to buy more fuel-efficient vehicles, along with tax penalties for buyers and users of SUVs (a combination increasingly talked about in public policy circles and referred to as a "feebate" system); subsidies for inherently unprofitable rural bus companies; or gas vouchers for the rural poor operating under a government-funded system akin to food stamps and WIC. These are all proposals now being floated in much of Western Europe. In the absence of such interventions, the costs of individual transportation will destroy all the careful financial calculations and penny-pinching balancing acts that provide the basis for so many low-income lives in today's America.

Nearly three years after Katrina sent U.S. oil prices soaring, I returned to Siskiyou County. By May 2008, gas stations around the regions were charging over four dollars for a gallon of regular unleaded—from $4.01 at Manfred's Food and Gas Depot just off Interstate 5 in Dunsmuir to over $4.15 in many other locales. And pretty much everyone was expecting—as, in fact, occurred—prices to keep heading north. A month later, gas prices in some remoter parts of California were dallying with the five dollar mark; and, while prices then collapsed in the months following, long-term indicators were that once the economy began to recover they would jag higher again, settling on a new plateau higher than the one they had occupied just a couple years earlier.

In combination with the collapsing housing market and the growing credit squeeze, the high gas prices of the post-Katrina years were throwing America into a recession, with businesses raising prices on goods and services, and laying off workers. For the first time in a generation, pundits were talking of an economy squeezed by stagflation, a lethal combination of rising prices—mostly triggered by the soaring cost of energy—and rising unemployment. In the first part of 2008, however, before banks and investment institutions started tumbling, the recession was mainly confined to blue-collar America and rural America. Thus, even while areas like Siskiyou County were being hammered (throughout much of the rural and desert regions of California, Bureau of Labor Statistics data showed that unemployment had risen above 9 percent by mid-2008) into the late summer of that year economists were still debating whether the country as a whole had fallen into a recession.

By mid-2008 high gas prices impacted middle-class Americans' holiday planning and weekend trips; among the invisible working poor, however, they triggered the onset of a siege mentality. People were only driving into town once or twice a month for groceries, many had stopped going out evenings, and they were only rarely driving to see friends and family. People who had bought natural gas or propane heating systems a few years earlier could no longer afford to heat their houses—or, if they could, it was only because they were getting their food from local pantries instead of buying it—and many were reverting to using old wood-fired stoves.

Over four thousand people received donations from the Yreka Food Ministry's distribution center, behind the city's probation offices, in 2007. The staff expected this number to rise through 2008. By the summer of that year, close to thirteen hundred mothers were getting free milk, cheese, eggs, beans, and peanut butter for their children from the local WIC program, a large increase over the previous year; even some of the county sheriffs' deputies were now deemed to be poor enough to qualify for WIC. (In Idaho, a similar story held; there, food banks reported that low-paid teachers were accessing their services in some small towns as high gas prices hit home.) In Dunsmuir, so many children began coming to school hungry that the school started giving out free breakfasts to every student. And, throughout the region, food pantries were reporting new clients: the working poor—hotel maids, gas station attendants, and fast-food restaurant workers, to name a few—were now simply unable to put food on their own tables without assistance.

Siskiyou's residents were hunkering down, hoping and praying for the gas storm to blow over. And, until it did, they had little choice but to drive themselves toward fiscal ruin.

Between 2000 and 2008, oil prices quadrupled. The ripple effects of this second great oil shock will affect global economic systems for years to come.

By July 2008, oil was trading at $147 a barrel on the London and New York markets, and many analysts were predicting a rush toward the $200 mark. The high energy prices were at least in part responsible for the resulting financial collapse. Banks started to fail because so many people defaulted on their variable-rate subprime mortgages. Secondary institutions that had bought these "mortgage securities" then started to fail because investors worried they were holding worthless paper and started cashing out while they still could. But one of the main reasons low-income Americans went into arrears so quickly on these loans—finding themselves unable to make their monthly payments pretty much immediately rather than a year or two after the variable rates kicked in—was that high energy prices had entirely corroded their rainy day funds.

In remote regions like Siskiyou County, something as basic as getting to the doctor had suddenly become a budget buster. Even if you were lucky enough to have the best health insurance plan in the world, the numbers still weren't in your favor if you had to burn up a half tank of four-dollar-a-gallon gas to visit your doctor each week. In Siskiyou County it was common to have to spend twenty to thirty dollars on gas for the round trip to see a specialist—and this in a region where jobs paying ten and eleven dollars per hour, with $150 taken out of your check every two weeks for health insurance premiums, were considered plum employment opportunities. Rosie Kerr had a friend who was eating up her savings just on the gas to get to Medford each week for her dialysis.

Similar stories could be heard all over the country. In Boise City, Oklahoma, Phyllis Burdick, a retired woman on Social Security, had even tried to pick up bit-work as a babysitter to pay for the gas to drive her sick husband down to Amarillo, Texas. "It's getting worse. We're trying to make ends meet. My husband's diabetic, only has one eye—and it's not very good. He can't work. I tried to babysit. [She earned two dollars per hour.] But it got too much, what with taking him to the doctor. So I stopped. We just live on our Social [Security], do the best we can. I help here [at the food pantry]; and, yes, I get food also." It was, she admitted sadly, the first time in her life she'd had to resort to charity. "It's been six months. I take my husband to the doctor in Amarillo, one hundred twenty miles from here. That's half a tank of gas. We go once or twice a month. Just went down and he had an artery cleaned out in his neck. But we survive. We survive." *How much money did the Burdicks have saved up?* "We have enough put away to bury us. That's what we keep it for—to bury us. And we live on fifteen hundred dollars a month."

In a world of low energy costs, the web of risky subprime securities would still have eventually unraveled—it was, after all, a fundamentally unsound business model, and like all bubbles at some point it had to pop—but it might have done so at a slower, more manageable pace. Instead, the situation spiraled down so quickly that by early October 2008 policy makers were openly talking of the possibility of a global financial meltdown, the onset of deflation instead of high inflation, and a decade-long depression; and central governments around the globe were desperately pumping trillions of dollars into the financial system to keep it from collapse.

As America's economic growth skidded to a halt in the autumn of 2008, and Europe, too, headed toward recession, as Asian exporter nations saw their overseas markets drying up and began slowing their own production levels, suddenly oil prices did a U-turn. Within five months of reaching their $147 per barrel peak price, they were down to under forty dollars, a level less than 30 percent of what they had been in July.

Good news for consumers, right? Well, not really. Like all the other markets caught up in this particular financial panic, the oil market collapsed on the fear that the global economy would implode, at least in part as a result of the stresses caused by years of high energy costs. Oil demand fell largely because the United States started shedding jobs at a startling rate. By October 2008, with the stock market losing 40 percent of its value and with global credit markets gridlocked, twenty-one states had unemployment rates of at least 6 percent. Illinois had 7.3 percent unemployment, California 8.2 percent, and Michigan 9.3 percent. By December 2008, another half-million-plus jobs had disappeared, the Big Three car companies were teetering on the edge of collapse, financial companies such as Bank of America were announcing layoffs for tens of thousands of employees, and many states were running out of funds to pay unemployment benefits to their jobless populations. Nationally, in the span of one year, unemployment had risen from 4.9 to 6.7 percent. In just three months—September, October, and November of 2008—the economy had shed over 1.25 million jobs. Millions more—jobless but no longer actively looking for work—were not counted in the unemployment data. And for those with work, the average number of hours worked per week was down to 33.5, the lowest level ever recorded by the Bureau of Labor Statistics.

All signs suggested that these numbers—of the unemployed and the jobless—were going to continue to rise for many months, if not years to come, with many economists predicting a long period of double-digit unemployment. After months in which economists debated whether or not the country was actually in a recession, now the debate was about whether or not it would actually slip into a depression, characterized by a sharp contraction in output and wealth, then a long period of stagnant growth and high unemployment.

In fact, following on the heels of the collapse in energy costs came the rare spectacle of *declining* retail prices and the entirely unpleasant specter of deflation. Companies could only move their products by slashing prices—but in slashing prices they were also reducing their ability to raise enough money to continuing paying all their workers. All of this was making a bad employment situation even worse. And who cares about cheap oil if nobody can afford to buy cars or maintain the ones they already have, if oil-using industries are idled and money flows dammed up? Moreover, a peek below the surface revealed that declining oil prices hardly seemed to represent a stable new equilibrium. Periodically, throughout the price decline, there were short-term spikes in the price of oil: Once it became clear that international leaders would pretty much spend whatever it took to keep the banking system afloat, for example, oil prices began a short march north again. On October 13, 2008, the day stock markets around the world posted one of the largest ever one-day rallies—raising hopes, unjustified it later turned out, that markets had bottomed out—oil prices rose by nearly 5 percent. Then the markets sank once more, and with them—as expectations of a global recession-cum-depression grew again—the price of crude oil. Two weeks later, on October 28, amid rumors of an imminent Federal Reserve interest rate cut, the Dow Jones roared back to life with a 10 percent gain; and for the first time in days crude oil prices also rose, up 2.5 percent during a few hours of frenetic early afternoon trading.

If, over the coming years, the financial system recovers and global growth resumes, it's a pretty safe bet that oil prices will again ricochet higher. And if the injection of cash into the banking system doesn't ultimately work, well, in an era of widespread, long-term deflation, cheap oil will be at best a marginal consolation.

It's a truly epic dilemma: we need economic growth, but the current energy order means that that growth leads not just to predictable, slow-moving oil price increases but to rapid, unpredictable jags in price. And those jags, recent experience shows, can be of a sufficient magnitude to throw the lives of millions and the workings of entire financial systems into turmoil. Yet the only way to avoid the surging prices is to take the global economy into a deflationary nosedive, which no sane policy maker wants to do. Tight oil supplies make it ever harder to create durable economic recoveries at the back end of recessions and evermore likely that those recoveries will rapidly sow the seeds of their own destruction, putting the world economy into a series of catastrophic gyrations between stagflation, on the one hand, and deflation on the other.

Price caps during periods of tight supply won't solve this particular problem. All that will happen is a lot of Americans will be left driving big, gas-guzzling vehicles, the world market will not be able to provide enough oil to U.S. consumers at prices they can readily afford, and consumers will be waiting in long lines for what limited oil there is. Price caps were tried in the 1970s and failed dismally. Cap the price that can be charged for a vital commodity and you seed a potent black market. And despite Republican Party chants of "drill, baby, drill" during the 2008 presidential election season, opening up protected areas of Alaska or California's shoreline to oil exploration won't cure this particular malaise, either. Even if America had enough untapped reserves to significantly alter market price calculations—and it doesn't—American consumers wouldn't have exclusive access to the extra barrels of black gold. The U.S. oil industry is run by private companies, so any oil they produce would go into the global market rather than be reserved for American consumers. The global price might fall marginally as a result, but growing demand in India and China would likely cancel out any such price reduction within a short period of time. In other words, given the realities of today's energy markets, when prices are high, America's options for reducing at-the-pump prices for consumers are limited. And when prices are low, it's as likely as not due to the broader global economy being in a serious recession, thereby canceling out the economic benefits to consumers of low prices.

Neither can these problems be solved by letting the market operate unfettered or by imposing heavy-handed regulations, such as price caps. Instead, what the current energy crisis demands is for the government to be aggressively committed to creative solutions.

In addition to massive investments in green energy technology in the arenas of power generation, home heating, and hybrid, electric, and fuel cell vehicles, as well as in improvements in the nation's public transport infrastructure, there's an immediate need for targeted tax rebates for passenger vehicles and personal transport.

At the same time, Washington should consider establishing an equivalent of the food stamps program for poor rural residents who have no choice but to drive to work. A gas stamp program could be designed as a temporary measure during transition into a green energy future. The average life of a car in the United States is estimated to be between seventeen and nineteen years; one option would be to create a twenty-year gas stamp program designed to help people navigate higher gas prices until the current generation of cars has largely run through the system and been replaced by more fuel-efficient vehicles.

An outlandish idea? No more so than energy subsidies for low-income Americans so that they don't go cold during winter or swelter in dangerously hot dwellings during summer. The Low Income Home Energy Assistance Program (LIHEAP), begun in 1981, channels federal dollars to the states, which then distribute the money to needy residents. The exact amount varies from year to year, but in recent years it has averaged out at about $2 billion. Each state creates its own eligibility standards, and each state maintains its own list of recipients. A federal gas stamp program could create its own client lists, or, for speedier implementation, states could duplicate their LIHEAP lists, working on the assumption that most low-income residents who need help heating their homes also need help filling their cars to drive to work or into town to pick up food. To qualify, people already on the LIHEAP list would simply need to provide proof that they own a car. Once qualified, individuals would either receive a monthly check to cover some of their gas costs or receive gas purchase cards, valued at, say, twenty gallons of gas per month. In the same way that supermarkets take food stamps in lieu of cash, gas stations would be obligated to take gas stamps from low-income drivers.

Unlike an across-the-board gas price subsidy, of the kind that allows motorists in Iran or Venezuela, say, to fill up their tanks for a mere few dollars, or that protects consumers in India or Malaysia from bearing the full brunt of market changes, a gas stamp program would not distort the market. No incentive would be built in for Americans to overconsume a scarce natural resource; instead, it would allow a targeted sliver of the population to continue buying enough gas to get to work, visit the doctor, or drive into town to go to the supermarket without busting holes in their family budgets.

A version of this proposal was, in fact, put forward in July 2008 by Representative Jim McDermott, a Democratic congressman from Washington State, who was, at the time, chairman of the House Ways and Means Subcommittee on Income Security and Family Support. McDermott's legislation, titled the Emergency Gasoline Assistance Act, would have channeled $5 billion in subsidies to low-income Americans. But the plan, which did not get voted on before the November election, would have worked simply by giving every state a one-time grant from the federal government, to disburse to poverty-line households as a gas stamp subsidy. How that money was then allocated would have depended on the whims of state legislators. Moreover, because McDermott didn't propose ongoing funding for the program, it would have served more as a singular tax rebate than as a food stamp–type extension of the social safety net.

A better idea would be to enact a multiyear gas stamp program as part of a larger fiscal stimulus package, with trigger prices built into the bill. It could, for example, remain dormant until gas hits $2.50 per gallon, in 2008 dollars, in a given state. Once the subsidy mechanisms are activated, their value could be tied to the average cost over a three-month period with the value of the gas stamps allocated to an eligible recipient rising each time that average increased by another fifty cents per gallon.

Such a program would only make sense environmentally if, in lockstep with it, the federal administration worked to make the U.S. vehicle fleet more fuel efficient. Though government shouldn't absolutely regulate what sorts of vehicles can be driven, politicians should use tax and subsidy instruments, and regulatory controls, to the maximum extent possible. Regulatory powers should be invoked to drastically increase vehicle fleet fuel-efficiency standards, and a target should be set to have a majority of passenger vehicles run on hybrid, fuel cell, or electric technology within the decade.

Technologically, the move into an economy no longer so reliant on oil is possible; what's needed is the political will to nudge the market in this direction. In the past, politicians have been reluctant to rock the cheap-oil boat by implementing such changes. In an era of high gas prices and accelerating global warming, that reluctance has waned. President Obama campaigned on a promise of investing $150 billion in new energy technologies over a ten-year period. His economics team developed the idea of subsidizing auto companies' health-care obligations to their retirees in exchange for those companies investing in the development of non–gas dependent vehicles. He called for raising average fuel-efficiency standards to forty miles per gallon within the decade, and he put forward the goal of reducing U.S. oil consumption by over one-third during this same time frame. "When John F. Kennedy decided that we were going to put a man on the moon," Obama declared, "he didn't put a bounty out for some rocket scientist to win—he put the full resources of the U.S. government behind the project and called on the ingenuity and innovation of the American people."

At the same time that large infrastructure changes are implemented, federal and state taxation policy should be altered to help shape more environmentally savvy, less oil-saturated consumer preferences on an individual level. After all, while we like to think of our consumption preferences as purely personal, nobody consumes in a vacuum. We are all, to one degree or another, creatures of our social contexts. That means that fuel-efficient and hybrid cars ought to come with ongoing tax incentives attached; not just a one-year tax rebate the year the car is purchased, but a rebate for each year the car is driven. It also means that large gas-guzzlers, especially sports utility vehicles (SUVs), should come with hefty tax penalties. That still would leave the SUV legal, but it would come with a higher sticker price, reflecting the broader social cost borne by society when gas-guzzlers contribute to tightening the oil supply and push the cost of gas up for everybody else. France implemented such a system in 2007, and as of 2008 an increasing number of British politicians were also coming out in favor of such a reform.

Finally, the federal government should consider releasing money to localities and states to implement local SUV buyback policies, somewhat akin to the handgun buyback policies put in place in several cities since April 1999. At that time, the federal government released $15 million in funds to help get guns off the streets of big cities. Progressive think tanks, such as the D.C.-based Center for American Progress, have favored such a move for several years. The Internet search engine giant Google included such a proposal in an ambitious plan it developed to wean Americans off oil. And a small but vocal minority of environmentally savvy economists has come up with similar ideas over the past few years. "Here's an example of how a Cash for Clunkers program might work," Princeton economist Alan Blinder wrote in the *New York Times* in July 2008. "The government would post buying prices, perhaps set at a 20 percent premium over something like Kelley Blue Book prices, for cars and trucks above a certain age (say, 15 years) and below a certain maximum value (perhaps $5,000). A special premium might even be offered for the worst gas-guzzlers and the worst polluters." Blinder continued by arguing that "the government can either sell the cars it buys to licensed recyclers for scrap, or refit them with new emissions controls and resell them. But the government must not ship the cars to poor countries, where they would continue to belch pollutants."

A national "scrappage" program of this sort was advocated by the U.S. Department of Transportation as far back as 2003, but two years later lobbyists for the auto industry convinced Congress to bar federal funding for any such program. Several states, including California, Illinois, Texas, and Virginia, do operate limited scrappage programs to get cars that fail local smog tests off the roads, but the numbers are small and the programs don't generally include cars that may be large and fuel inefficient but nevertheless pass pollution tests.

Today there's a need for more ambitious scrappage programs. As gas prices soared in 2007–8, the bottom fell out of the secondhand market for big cars, with SUV resale values plunging by a quarter or more in the first half of 2008. Many owners found they couldn't sell their vehicles no matter how low they dropped the price. Thus, many low-income people, such as Neal Owen, who bought gas-guzzlers back when gas was $1.50 a gallon, were driving to financial ruin in vehicles they could no longer afford to drive but couldn't sell, either. Even when prices dipped back below two dollars again in the late fall of 2008, the SUV market remained subdued, at least in part because people feared the declining cost of gas was only a temporary blip in an energy landscape that was likely to lead to higher prices over the long run.

To help Owen and others move toward driving less fuel-greedy vehicles, the government may ultimately have to step into the fray. This could work in several ways: Sell your SUV to a licensed dealer at the going market rate, and the government would kick in an extra amount of money, say one thousand dollars. Sell it for scrap, and the government would add in enough money to pay the first two or three payments on a fuel-efficient vehicle. Or donate it to charity and the government would, say, double or even triple the value of the tax deduction. None of these proposals would completely flush the SUV problem out of the American vehicle fleet, but all would speed the process along.

In the absence of some kind of policy intervention, more and more regions will face the sort of impossible math confronting Siskiyou County and its residents, and the social unrest seen in much of the world in response to rising energy costs. In Europe, where gas and diesel prices soared to twelve and even thirteen dollars a gallon in some countries by the summer of 2008, truckers blockaded ports and fuel depots to protest escalating diesel costs. One trucker died when he was run over by a vehicle trying to cross a protestors' picket line. Riots broke out in reaction to rising food and fuel prices in parts of Asia, civil servants demonstrated in India, and there were large street protests in South Korea. In Tunisia security forces shot into crowds protesting rising oil prices, and in Bolivia construction workers struck to protest the rising costs. In the United States, by mid-2008, tens of thousands of independent truckers were going out of business, thousands of big-rigs were being idled, and independent truckers' associations were warning of serious upheaval without government intervention. Indeed, during the spring of 2008, truckers protested in Pennsylvania, Washington, D.C., and ports in Florida, Georgia, and Washington State.

"The effect of diesel prices going up effects everyone in some way," Noreta Taylor, executive director of the Owner-Operator Independent Drivers Association, based out of Grain Valley, Missouri, explained. "When you have diesel prices rising, and if shippers are having to pay more, they're going to charge more for their goods."

By mid-2008, as the energy crunch peaked, independent truckers were spending up to one thousand dollars more per week on diesel for their five-mile-per-gallon rigs compared to a year or two earlier. Some of that was being passed onto customers; much of it, however, the truckers were having to absorb—and it was literally driving them into bankruptcy. When oil prices started heading north, the United States had about 400,000 independent truckers on its highways. In the first three months of 2008 alone, one thousand trucking companies, representing about 42,000 trucks, went out of business. For those truckers who managed to stay afloat, Taylor estimated the higher diesel prices were reducing their disposable income by between one-third and one-half. Some had begun working second jobs to meet these extra expenses; others were temporarily idling their trucks; still others were looking to get out of the business altogether.

"People are having so much trouble with fuel and overhead, they can't do it anymore," one-time trucker Roy Gouveia explained, as he stood in line at the Fort Jones food pantry. "You can't even afford to be an owner-operator anymore. What I always said, when the trucker stops in this country, oh boy, watch out! Everything's got to go on trucks."

■ ■ ■

Interlude I

It is an eternal obligation toward the human being not
to let him suffer from hunger when one has a chance
of coming to his assistance.
—SIMONE WEIL*

Sacramento's main food bank is housed in a large brick building on
the edge of Oak Park, one of the city's poorest neighborhoods. It
shares the premises with a clothing bank, a nutritional education
center, and various other social service programs. Every day, supermarkets and restaurants donate surplus, often outdated foods; community residents drive up and drop off bags; and sometimes farmers
come in with extra produce. Inside the warehouse, a small staff—
backed up by a network of volunteers—sort through the large quantities of donated food, divide it into categories—breads, vegetables,
sweets, dairy, miscellaneous, USDA (canned vegetables, pasta, some
canned fruit), cereal, ramen noodles—and prepare for the rush
of hungry folks who start lining up each morning long before ten
o'clock, when the food bank officially opens.

About sixty thousand people a year receive food from Sacramento's
three largest food banks, and several thousand more receive help
from smaller pantries and emergency soup kitchens. In a busy week,
the main food bank alone will provide food for several thousand

*French philosopher and political activist Simone Weil starved herself to
death during World War II to protest the conditions faced by the populace
of occupied France.

local residents. To one pantry, in the affluent suburb of Elk Grove, comes the young single mother who works at a local brewery but doesn't bring home enough to pay all her bills. To another comes a temporarily out-of-work oil-tanker driver. There's a Filipino home helper, a Mexican construction worker, a retired couple from the Ukraine. Economic conditions forced them all to choose between paying the rent, buying gas, paying utility bills, accessing medical care, or purchasing food.

Until the middle of this past decade, most of these people never had to rely on any kind of public welfare or private charity. These "new hungry" turn up at food banks, embarrassed and unsure of themselves, looking for a bit of help to tide them over until their next paycheck. The free food they get is supposed to last three days; many make it stretch a week or more.

"I've never been on assistance in my whole life," said the tanker driver shamefacedly. "I can't think of a word to describe it. Embarrassing. But you've got to swallow your pride when your kids need to eat. I got a four-bedroom, three-bath, two-story in a court. I got three cars. It happens to everybody. Sometimes it just happens." The driver had recently separated from his wife, and the burdens of paying all his family's bills on one income tipped him over the edge. He had assets, just no ready cash to buy his weekly groceries.

"We think of the homeless as the face of hunger," Eileen Thomas, executive director of River City Community Services, explained. "But the face of hunger is children in apartment complexes, people who come from minimum-wage jobs, people who live on SSI or general assistance, or senior citizens." For years Thomas had been working with hungry Sacramentans. Recently, she had found that many of them were employees—at McDonald's and Wal-Mart, in hotels, and as housecleaners.

Census Bureau data backs up Thomas's hunch that a lot of working poor are struggling to make it in her city. In Sacramento County, as of 2007, 5.1 percent of residents were living on income less than half the federally defined poverty level, and fully 6.2 percent of the region's quarter-million-plus part-time workers fell into this income bracket. Another 4 percent lived on or just above the poverty threshold. In the following year, Sacramento—like most of the rest of the country—saw that data go from bad to far worse.

Old and young, black, white, Latino, Asian, the clients line up in the narrow, enclosed corridor that snakes along the edge of the food bank. Some are mumbling or shouting, clearly mentally distressed; others come with their children, down on their luck and just looking for a break. When they reach the Plexiglas slide windows, they present their IDs and the IDs of all the members of their household for whom they are claiming food. A case manager keys into the database, double-checking that they haven't been served within the past thirty days; then the client fills in a form: name, address, date of birth. The manager circles the number of adults and children in the household and whether or not they qualify for USDA food—they have to live within a certain service area to receive this—in addition to that donated by private sources.

Then they sit on the metal benches by the gray wall and wait, passively hoping for decent pickings.

Inside the food bank, a bizarre inversion of roles takes place. The volunteers—many of them local retirees, some of them workers from nearby companies that encourage their employees to do charity work—pick up flattop, hard-to-wheel shopping carts carrying cardboard boxes and fistfuls of plastic bags, swing by the case manager's basket to take the filled-in forms, and proceed to go "shopping." That's what they call it. They look at how many people they are shopping for, see how old the person who has filled in the form is, try to gauge their ethnicity and perhaps their food preferences from their name, and set to work.

Everyone gets a mystery bag of miscellaneous donated produce. Everyone gets one ramen noodle package per person in the home. Everyone gets at least one loaf of bread and, most days, a minimum amount of fruits and/or vegetables. On a good day it will be peppers, strawberries, even California artichokes. On a bad day, just sacks of wilting shredded cabbage. And almost everyone gets a small bag of USDA produce. But then the discretion kicks in. Do they have kids in the household? If so, let's try to find a nice gooey cake with sickly sweet icing on top, or some sprinkle-covered cupcakes. Make sure the ones with kids get milk—hopefully not too far past the sell-by date—and eggs. If a few donated roasted chickens are sitting on a table, grab them for the bigger families. If there are a couple bags of vacuum-packed fish, make sure the ones with young kids get them. If you are "shopping" for an old couple, try to keep it simple: canned soups, cottage cheese, maybe a nice bag of bagels. If you're shopping for someone homeless, avoid food that has to be cooked. As the hours go by, and more people continue to arrive, you start imagining stories, trying to guess who these men and women are and why they're here.

I think of my grandparents' kitchen, the pound cakes and simple biscuits, the strudels and sweet rolls; and, when I see an old lady quietly sitting and waiting for her food, I "shop" for her as I would for my grandparents. No gooey donuts all stuck together, no massive icing-topped monstrosities; nothing too messy or sweet. Instead, I go for the simple pastries—cinnamon rolls, cherry pies, the sorts of things you can share with old friends while chatting over a long cup of coffee. I throw in a nice stick of French bread. I try to add in an orange juice, just to help keep her healthy. It must be miserable being old and hungry and sick all at once. I see a sad-looking middle-aged man, his face full of defeat, and rummage around the "miscellaneous" table looking for chocolate bars to throw into the box. I dive into the huge tub of yogurts and milks and cottage cheeses, all mixed together, many smeared with bright berry yogurt from leaking containers. I look for produce less than a week past sell-by and add them to his box.

All around the warehouse, volunteers are performing similar

shopping feats. When the boxes are filled, the volunteers wheel the carts to another Plexiglas window. They unlatch the shut mechanism and slide the window open. They call out a first name, wait for the person to walk up, then ask for their last name or date of birth. You've got to be careful you've got the right person; you never know who will try to scam you for a bigger box than they're entitled to. Some of the volunteers seem slightly embarrassed by this part of the process; others, including one ramrod retired military man in his eighties, take it extremely seriously. He calls out a name, watches until the man or woman is right at his window, then barks out, "Last name? Address? What's your date of birth?" It's a test. Get it wrong, he's saying, and you get no food. Not on his watch. A watery-eyed old woman, who acts like she has never been to the food bank before— nervous, embarrassed, not quite sure where to sit or how to act—asks to borrow a box to carry her bags to her car. Ramrod gets extremely irate. You can't do this, he tells her; you might *steal* the box.

I wheel my cart up to the window to give food to a woman who looks like she's in her fifties. *Please*, she says aggressively, *can I have a raspberry cake? And some juice?* I have to temper my annoyance. *Who does she think she is?* a not-particularly-charitable voice inside me cries out. *She's getting all this free stuff and yet demanding more and insisting on certain kinds of food.* But when I reluctantly agree, and return to the window with her desired extras, her face cracks open into an extraordinary grin, and she practically cries with joy. This, I realize, had precious little to do with the specific food items and everything to do with pride, with her needing to be able to assert just a tiny degree of autonomy amid the humiliation. For her, asking for, and getting, the cake and juice allowed her to say, "I am someone."

I wish her a good day, and slide the window shut. You've got to slide it shut and lock it, just in case an irate customer decides to jump inside and shop for himself. I wheel my squeaky cart back to the front basket, pick up another form, and continue shopping.

TWO

When the Month Is Longer Than the Money

The poverty of our century is unlike that of any other. It is not, as poverty was before, the result of natural scarcity, but of a set of priorities imposed upon the rest of the world by the rich. Consequently, the modern poor are not pitied but written off as trash. The twentieth-century consumer economy has produced the first culture for which a beggar is a reminder of nothing.

—JOHN BERGER, "The Soul and the Operator,"
   Expressen (Stockholm, March 19, 1990)

BILLY MACPHERSON BELIEVED that for many of her friends and pantry clientele "the months are longer than the money." What little income they brought in each month—from work, from Social Security or disability checks, in food stamps or welfare payments— was never quite enough to last a full four-plus weeks. And so they faced an unpalatable choice: try to stretch the family budget to cover the whole month, which involved scrimping on food and missing meals throughout the entire period, or eat semi-decently for the first two or three weeks of the month and pray that something, somehow, would come about to tide them through the lean times at the end.

Once gas prices started going up, food prices also headed north— at least in part because so much corn and arable land was diverted into biofuel production in response to the energy crunch; in part, too, because oil-based fertilizers soared in price and inflation took root throughout the broader economy. In the last years of George W. Bush's presidency, that lean period at the end of each month began to grow. Instead of a few days, it became a week; then it became ten days, even two weeks. For low-income Americans, wages and government checks lagged far behind inflation, leaving them little choice but to watch as month after month their never particularly munificent purchasing power collapsed.

In the years following 2005, as the price of staples such as wheat and rice more than doubled, deadly food riots broke out in Bangladesh, Haiti, Cameroon, Yemen, Mexico, Egypt, Burkina Faso, and several other countries. People earning one or two dollars a day were facing starvation caused not by drought or plagues of locusts but by the workings of the international commodities market. In some nations, governments were brought to their knees by the disturbances; in others, panicked ministers met in emergency sessions to limit crop exports and try to shore up their populaces' food supplies.

By 2008 America's impoverished classes were, albeit to a lesser extent, facing a similar price-induced hunger. Unlike the destitute of countries such as Ethiopia and the Sudan, who too often went hungry because crops failed and what little food there was got bought up by their richer neighbors, America's poor were being priced out of a market flush with excess eatables. Theirs was a hunger amid plenty, an inability to buy their way to seats at the most food-laden table in history. At the same time as hungry Milwaukee residents—on false rumors of free food deliveries—were fighting each other for access to hoped-for supplies in the spring of 2008, at the same time as immigrant shoppers in many neighborhoods were stampeding to buy up large bags of rice in the face of rising prices, hot dog–eating and fried asparagus–eating competitions were gaining in popularity from the Coney Island boardwalk in New York to the agricultural town of

Stockton, California. One visit to any of these binge-eating orgies would have been enough to put paid to the notion that American hunger, twenty-first-century style, was in any way about the country as a whole facing food shortages. Yes, food prices were rising, but they were rising due to increased energy costs and growing global demand for American food exports rather than in response to a collapse in the nation's food supply. The country's growing epidemic of hunger was less a symptom of food market contractions and more one of the stealth spread of poverty and inflation into more and more corners of American life.

The U.S. government's official poverty line in 2008 was $10,590 for a single person, $13,540 for a couple, $16,530 for a family of three, and $21,203 for a family of four. And the Census Bureau estimated that over 37 million Americans (including noncitizen residents) were living at or below these income levels. But that only hinted at the growing scale of American poverty. Economists such as Bob Pollin, codirector of the Political Economy Research Institute at the University of Massachusetts, believed many tens of million Americans more were living on incomes that, while they might meet a denuded government "minimum-wage" threshold, in reality couldn't be expected to meet a family's basic needs.

Pollin's team calculated that a single person needed to earn ten dollars an hour to achieve even a semblance of economic security; and, as with the poverty line, so with this measure, which he called a "living wage," the dollar amount would go up as the number of people in the family increased.

Guaranteeing a living wage was an ambitious goal, one that a number of localities had been trying to implement since the mid-1990s, when Baltimore's city council passed a limited living-wage bill that impacted about fifteen hundred local workers employed by companies who did business with the city. And nowhere were such local measures more of a hot-button issue than in Santa Fe, New Mexico.

In the late winter of 2006, Santa Fe's then-mayor David Coss sat behind his large desk discussing the city's living wage, his long, wiry body draped in an expensive gray-brown linen suit, a cream shirt and dark-patterned tie, his hair neatly coiffed, his graying goatee smartly trimmed. A Georgia O'Keefe poster of a horned animal's skull hung on the wall behind him. A second poster, in pastels, showed off a glorious Southwestern desert and mountain landscape—a world of swirling dreams and endless possibilities. Coss had a background as an environmental scientist and a union organizer; he had risen to power at City Hall at least in part because of his assertive championing of the most comprehensive living-wage statute in America.

Three years earlier, after a decade-long campaign by social justice activists, seven of the eight councilmen in the chic—and expensive— desert town voted to raise the city's minimum wage to $8.50 an hour, with successive increases built in that would hike it up to $10.50 by 2008. In the years following, despite litigation from opponents of a living wage, the courts rejected challenges to the law, and public support for the change remained high—notwithstanding doom and gloom prognostications from the town's tourism-dominated service industries. Santa Fe's living wage was, Coss averred, "basic economic fairness in making the economy work for everyone and not just the people at the top." When the chamber of commerce ran candidates against the four councillors most outspoken in their support of the living wage, the chamber's candidates were all soundly beaten on Election Day.

In a town with a high percentage of practicing Catholics, the living wage in Santa Fe was pushed not just as a sensible economic move—as a way to stimulate spending and savings cycles along the bottom edge of the labor market—but as a moral imperative, reinforced by the authority of papal encyclicals dating back to Leo XIII at the tail end of the nineteenth century. "No one who works full time should have to live in poverty," Monsignor Jerome Martinez stated. The monsignor was a middle-aged man with a shock of curly gray hair, a warm smile, and a deeply suntanned, slightly pocked face. He shared his cluttered office in an annex to the spectacular Cathedral of St. Francis with two large green cacti and several oil paintings of Jesus. "The dignity of the worker is more than just being a cog in the industrial machine. The Just Wage provides sustenance, housing, minimum health care, retirement benefits, and that the worker should have an opportunity to be generous. The *ability* to be generous is an important aspect of the church. It makes you feel more like a human being." Smiling broadly, Martinez proudly recalled that, at a time when living-wage advocates dreamt of the $8.50 earnings floor, the church in Santa Fe paid none of its sixty-five employees less than $11.50 per hour.

Santa Fe's move followed that of dozens of other municipalities in the decade since Baltimore kick-started the process in 1994. By the turn of the century, over sixty cities had followed Baltimore's lead. And, in the years following, dozens more enacted such laws. In some cases, the living wage affected only city workers or businesses that contracted with city and state governments; elsewhere, they applied across the board. Yet, despite the movement's progress, it remained marginal, enforced in a few scores of cities but not adopted by even one state. California's statewide minimum wage, the highest in the country, was $8 an hour in 2008, still far short of what living-wage advocates claimed was needed to stabilize the lives of low-income workers. And in much of the country, a federal minimum wage prevailed. It was set at $5.15 an hour in 1997 and stayed at that level for ten years, its real value reduced by almost half, leaving recipients with less purchasing power than minimum-wage earners had had at any point in the previous half century. A new Democratic congressional majority finally passed a three-step minimum-wage increase in 2007; yet the increase envisaged only a $7.25 minimum wage by 2009, and it wasn't inflation indexed. Consequently, the federal minimum wage remained a woefully inadequate method of fighting poverty.

That the minimum wage became so diluted hinted at profound

changes within the nation's political culture. In 1938, Franklin Roosevelt signed the minimum wage into law, calling for a "fair day's pay for a fair day's work" and declaring that goods produced in workplaces that did not pay a minimum wage "should be regarded as contraband." Seventy years on, the minimum wage had lost close to half its real value and was seen as a political punching bag, attacked by conservative critics as impeding the workings of the free market.

By the early twenty-first century, reformers questing after Roosevelt's vision had come to accept that any minimum wage passed at the federal level was likely to be inadequate to meet the needs of its recipients; instead, they opted to push for local and state living-wage ordinances.

The living-wage movement, however, has had only limited impact. While many states enacted a higher minimum wage than that mandated by the federal government in the years since 1997, none implemented one that genuinely met living-wage criteria. As a result, low-end wages continued to stagnate in a process exacerbated by the systemic underestimation of inflation, which allowed employers to minimize the pay raises they gave to employees. Thus, in a period of unprecedented corporate profits and rising worker productivity—up 2.5 percent per year during the 2000s—most working Americans experienced either stagnant real income or a fall in real income during the Bush presidency. Census Bureau numbers showed that the median household income for working-age households fell, in 2007 dollars, by $2,010 in the years from 2000 to 2007, the only economic cycle on record in which real income for American workers has fallen. For racial minorities, the trend was even worse: median income for blacks declined by over 5 percent during these years; for Hispanics the decline was 3.1 percent.

At the same time, the percentage of Americans, many of them employed, living below the poverty line steadily rose. In the absence of strong wage-protection laws, many employers continued to grievously underpay their employees. Indeed, Bob Pollin came up with a disturbing estimate of the extent of this problem: by the end of the Bush presidency, fully one in three American workers was earning below his living-wage benchmark.

These were the people—described by Princeton University sociologist Katherine Newman as "the missing class"—most impacted by soaring gas and food costs, people who in the best of times spent a higher proportion of their incomes on basic necessities than did any other part of the population. They were deemed by the government too affluent to qualify for food stamps, Medicaid, and the other welfare programs that collectively constituted the country's frayed safety net. And yet, once oil prices doubled and then doubled again, once the cost of a gallon of milk, a dozen eggs, a pound of rice ballooned, these men, women, and children were the ones left most exposed to destitution. By trying to keep their jobs, low-wage earners and their families were in many ways rendering themselves worse off than those who never had, or couldn't keep, paid employment and who therefore qualified for the maximum food stamp allotment and various other government subsidies.

Barack Obama campaigned on a promise to raise the minimum wage to $9.50 per hour by 2011; if he makes good on this promise as president, and indexes that minimum wage to inflation, America would finally come close to Roosevelt's dream of a minimum wage that provided genuine economic security. Given the severity of the financial crisis and subsequent recession, however, it is more than likely this goal will continue to be a promise deferred. For now, at least, local living-wage ordinances and laws targeting the wages of public sector employees and workers for mega-companies like Wal-Mart continue to offer the best hope for creating a safety net for America's most vulnerable workers.

In the run-down central Oregon town of Alvadore, Becky Darnall and her husband fit the near-poor profile perfectly. He worked as a cook at a restaurant in the nearby town of Springfield; she worked part time cleaning the house of her elderly neighbor. Their combined income came to about $30,000 per year. When nothing went wrong, it was enough to pay the rent on their ramshackle mobile home and buy food for their three young children and a nephew who lived with them. When unexpected bills intruded, however, the Darnalls found themselves with no spare cash and no food for the kids.

The unexpected occurred when Becky, who lacked medical insurance at the time, ended up in the emergency room in 2007 after a severe asthma attack. It happened again in 2008 when gas prices spiked and Becky's husband had to spend close to fifteen dollars a day to drive their old Chevy Blazer, with a malfunctioning engine that they could not afford to repair, to work and back. The family jumped through hoops to qualify for a small amount of food stamps, yet still couldn't put enough food on the table come the end of each pay cycle. They borrowed money from friends; when those sources dried up, they took out payday loans, which they then had to struggle mightily to pay off over the course of a year.

And so, with their credit dried up, the Darnalls, like an increasing number of their employed but impoverished neighbors in 2007 and 2008, turned to the once-a-month food pantry operated out of the large wooden Alvadore Christian Church, on one of their town's dusty little side streets. There they could lay claim to bread, muffins, applesauce, canned soups, canned vegetables, and other necessities. It was, Becky announced, "the difference between vegetable soup with macaroni thrown in and a real dinner."

By the summer of 2008, Oregon food pantries were reporting that the proportion of their clients belonging to a family with at least one member employed had gone up from 30 percent to nearly 50 percent. Although overall hunger in the state was down from a decade earlier, when Oregon posted some of the worst hunger statistics in the nation, the number of rural Oregonians who reported being hungry had steadily risen since the year 2000. By 2004, before the worst of the gas-price crunch hit, 13.6 percent of rural residents in the state were classified as being "food insecure." Although this data wasn't updated to reflect recent economic changes, anecdotal stories from food pantries around the state suggested the problem had noticeably worsened in the following years, even as donations to the state's food bank system had dwindled by 3 million pounds of food per year since 2005.

As was the case in so many other states around the country before the financial meltdown of 2008, unemployment in Oregon was low, but the jobs were no longer paying the bills. "For a lot of folks, the emergency food box system was set up to respond to family emergencies. Over the last eight to nine years, instead of emergencies, people are *relying* on food boxes to a greater extent. It's really becoming a supplement to incomes," explained Ryan McCambridge, director of the Linn-Benton County Food Share. "The biggest demographic is folks who have jobs and can't make enough to make ends meet." Many of the remaining clients were retirees, men and women on fixed incomes who had worked for decades in blue-collar jobs only to find their retirement income eroded by rising food prices and increased costs for prescription drugs.

"I have rent to pay, electricity to pay, telephone to pay, and the luxury of a TV to pay," explained eighty-three-year-old Helen Wagy, a food-pantry client in Corvallis, Oregon. Wagy, a widow who, like the Darnalls, lived in a mobile home, retired several years earlier, after working for thirty-five years as a laundress. Her total monthly income was a $912 Social Security check. Without the pantry, Wagy's friend, Roberta Coulter, added pithily, "I'd probably lose a lot of weight. Without them, I could make the Jell-O but I wouldn't have the fruit."

Half a continent away, the same math held true for Audrey Rivera, a volunteer and client at the Catholic Family Service's Amarillo Resource Center, a food pantry in the Texas panhandle. The pantry, which shared a building with parole services, a home-

less medical clinic, and various other social service agencies, gave
clients a monthly account with a certain amount of dollars in it,
then allowed them to "shop" for donated food up to the dollar
value of their account. In wheeling their shopping carts down the
aisles, choosing food, and then proceeding to a checkout counter
to have their eatables deducted from their account, the Resource
Center's hard-pressed customers preserved at least the illusion of
independence.

Rivera was a divorcée in her mid-sixties; she had six children,
twenty-three grandchildren, and fourteen great-grandkids. She had
survived one bout of cancer and was now, with what seemed like an
indomitable spirit, battling a second. For many years, Rivera had
worked as a baker at a local retirement home, bringing in enough
money to feed her children, but not enough to feed herself; so, like
many women in similar situations, she cooked for her kids, pre-
tended not to be hungry, and then scraped their leftovers onto her
plate after they had finished. Years later, they confided that they had
always known what she was doing, and had deliberately left food
on their plates for her to eat. She felt desperately ashamed that her
children had nurtured this secret for so long, and wept as they told
her of their memories.

Audrey hurt her back on the job in 1986, then suffered through
several surgeries before finally having to retire. Until her Social
Security kicked in in 2007, she was living on forty dollars a month
in food stamps, a small pension that was owed her deceased first
husband, and a disability payment sent her way by the Baptist
Convention. Those two checks came to $550 a month. When times
got really tough, she'd open her door mornings and find that anonymous neighbors had left paper bags full of food on her doorstep.

By the time I met Audrey, her Social Security had kicked in, and
she was receiving $1,217 a month—putting her above the poverty
line for a single person. The downside was that she had lost her SSI
and, with it, her free medicines. She now had more cash, but much

of it went straight to purchasing prescription drugs. So Audrey Rivera went grocery shopping at the Resource Center, relying on the goodwill of local donors to keep the shelves stocked with everything from canned soups to bread to frozen fish fillets. She helped cook meals for homebound clients and could be relied on to rustle up a stew or a bean dish, or bake a cake or cook some ribs for the holiday dinners sponsored by the Center. "A lot of people donate groceries. But times are getting harder," she worried. "It seems that God always comes through and we always manage to have something. What will happen when there's nothing? I don't know."

The same worry plagued sixty-two-year-old Sylvia Boyd, a widow with a staggering array of medical problems—diabetes, arthritis, dementia, high blood pressure, an enlarged heart, a malfunctioning thyroid—who wasn't old enough to qualify for Medicare, and who somehow had to find the money not just for medicines but also for feeding and clothing a teenage granddaughter who was currently living with her. "The doctor told me two or three years ago that I can't work. I was falling. I was driving a school bus and I fell several times off the bus, and on the bus, and at home. My memory's been going since I lost my husband. I got to a point I couldn't remember what street to turn on. The kids would help me out. I made it through five years. Then one day, I got real sick and I couldn't make the route. I quit working. I was sixty-two and could get Social Security."

Each month, in addition to her $850 Social Security check, Boyd received forty dollars worth of food from the Resource Center. Although it was supposed to be primarily a stopgap form of help, she made that food stretch the entire four weeks. "If you don't eat a lot, and you watch what you do and how you fix it, you can manage," she explained. "I can make it with just rice, or water, gravy, and bread if I have to. I do, once or twice a month. If it weren't for places like this, and these people, we would starve."

"There's definitely been an increase in demand for food recently," noted the Resource Center's coordinator, named Katherine Camp, a young woman recently graduated from college. In April 2008, the Center was providing food to 176 clients and their families. By July 2008, that number had risen to 229; and by the late summer it was heading up toward 250. "It's steadily climbing, especially with increases in the cost of living and gas. In Texas, an elderly person who applies for food stamps only qualifies for ten dollars a month of food stamps. It can buy a gallon of milk, a loaf of bread, and some eggs. And then they rely on us for everything else."

Census Bureau data released in August 2008 showed that one in six Texans and one in four Texas children were living below the poverty line, and more state residents were expected to fall into poverty as the country's economic situation continued to deteriorate. The state's food bank network reported an 11 percent increase in demand in the first months of 2008, and the state's food stamp offices reported hundreds of thousands more Texans were qualifying for government food aid. A recently released study of hunger in the Texas panhandle found that nearly half the food bank clients in Amarillo were forced to choose between buying food and paying their utility bills and heating fuel costs; nearly four out of ten couldn't pay for both food and rent; and one in three were juggling food and medical bills. In the first six months of 2008, Xcel Energy, the Texas panhandle's largest electricity supplier, cut off service to more than sixteen thousand delinquent customers in the panhandle and rural eastern New Mexico. That number was five thousand higher than during the same period a year earlier.

"If you're making six dollars, seven dollars an hour, you can't make ends meet. The downturn in the economy and the price of fuel—which in turn has driven up the price of food—has turned the face of hunger from people worrying about where the next meal is coming from to 'it's here and they *are* missing meals,'" said Zack Wilson, public relations officer for the High Plains Food Bank in Amarillo. He was sitting at his computer in an office cluttered with antihunger memorabilia, and listening to an opera podcast. "There is a problem with hunger, and it could very well be your next-door neighbor living in a nice house or the person next to you in the grocery store line. People don't necessarily wave a white flag and say they're hungry. There's a lot of shame in hunger. But the face of hunger in Amarillo is, unfortunately, growing. When I started working here three and a half years ago, I didn't think hunger existed. But you drive around certain areas here and you can see it—the way kids and adults are going into restaurants to ask for food; you see it on the street corners and in our kids' café program. We have four elementary schools on our East Side, and the numbers of children we feed are astounding. At one site we sometimes feed over one thousand kids a night. Monday through Friday. We had a cold snap here. It was in the teens. We had kids come in with shorts and T-shirts on. They were holey, literally, razor thin. Our volunteers asked why they were coming out in this cold weather. They said if they didn't come out they wouldn't have anything to eat."

By 2008, tens of millions of Americans who weren't officially classified as living below the poverty line were nonetheless finding it impossible to pay the bills and put food on their family tables. As for savings, to help families navigate the hard times, for the people Billy MacPherson helped, or for the "shoppers" pushing carts full of donated food down the aisles of the Amarillo Resource Center, saving dollars was as impossible as driving to the moon. From 2005 on, for the first time since the Great Depression, American families were, on average, spending more than they were bringing in. The country had what economists term a negative rate of savings. Some had simply gotten used to binge consumption, borrowing against home equity lines of credit during the plush years of the housing boom and then running up high-interest credit card balances when houses ceased to be viable ATMs. For most low-income Americans, however, the simple act of consuming enough to survive involved a continual dalliance with debt.

Billy's neighbors, and countless others like them around the country, weren't living high on the hog; they were simply struggling to get by. If they still had credit, they were rapidly burning through it by maxing out their credit cards, missing utility payments, tempting the repo-men to reclaim their unpaid-for cars. If they'd used up their legitimate credit, they were now utilizing payday loans (one of only a handful of boom industries in small-town and inner-city America these days), borrowing money for a few days here, a few days there, at extraordinary rates of interest. In 2005, the D.C.-based Center for Responsible Lending estimated that the fees and interest on a typical $325 payday loan ran to $52 every two weeks. A year later the center issued a report, *Financial Quicksand: Payday lending sinks borrowers in debt with $4.2 billion in predatory fees every year*, which documented payday loans with APRs as high as 443 percent. "By requiring full repayment within a short period of time (generally two weeks)," the authors wrote, "lenders compel payday borrowers to return again and again, renewing a loan for another large fee without being able to pay down the principal." In other words, once ensnared in the payday loan game, borrowers generally had to borrow to pay off the fees attached to their original loans, and then borrow again to cover the new fees. Researchers found that 99 percent of payday loan users had to borrow multiple times in any given year, racking up astronomical user fees in the process.

At the same time, more and more people who didn't have enough money to maintain balances in their bank accounts were using check cashing services, handing over as much as 10 percent of their paychecks simply for the privilege of converting it to usable cash. Ten percent of whites and fully a quarter of black and Latino adults had no bank accounts. For these men and women, high-fee check cashing was a daily fact of life. And as the credit crunch intensified in 2007 and 2008, monitors reported the rise of an even more nefarious industry: lenders in low-income neighborhoods were fronting desperate people money, at extreme rates of interest, using anticipated Earned Income Tax Credit (EITC) rebates from the government as collateral. Taken together, payday lenders, check cashing agencies, EITC lenders, and the growing number of pawn shops in hardscrabble America represented a sort of countercultural financial system, a brutally exploitative credit infrastructure for individuals and neighborhoods long shunned by traditional banks and credit agencies. From 2007 to 2008, as credit cards and banks adopted stricter lending criteria, the informal lending sector bloomed, growing a staggering 16 percent in one year.

"This is the way we live," explained Angelita, a fifty-four-year-old woman who was working as a security guard. She was raising four of her grandkids in the little town of Caldwell, Idaho, because their parents were in prison on drug charges. "I've never had anything new. I always live by hand-me-downs. I shop at secondhand stores. It's kind of hard for the kids. They see other kids and want to be like them. We don't live the same kind of lifestyle that people who have [money] live. It doesn't pan out. Not anymore. If you don't have two incomes it's very hard. I usually go to the food bank. They give me a little box. Now, it's even lesser, because the economy's shrunken everything. Before, they gave you a variety: corn, a little meat, in the summer, vegetables. Now it's just a couple of cans and that's about it. No milk. Bread sometimes. I borrow from my job or my mom until I get paid. They take it out of my check when I get paid. I'm just barely making it to go to work."

Similar stories could be found all over Caldwell. Tammera Mojica's family maxed out their credit cards, saw their house go into foreclosure during the subprime mortgage crisis, sold off family heirlooms on Craigslist, and had their car repossessed. They started trading in their kids' clothes at the local thrift store when the children grew and needed larger sizes, and finally filed for bankruptcy.

Tammera was a longtime student at Boise State University, and her husband worked as a furniture finisher for Best Bath. He earned about $30,00 a year, putting the family far enough above the poverty line that, while the kids qualified for WIC, they were unable to access food stamps. As their financial situation deteriorated, they had to start using payday loans to meet the bills. At one point they were paying thirty dollars in monthly "fees" for every one hundred dollars borrowed. The APR on payday loans in Idaho was 443 percent, according to the Center for Responsible Lending, lower than the 574 percent APR allowed in Wisconsin, the 560 percent charged in Louisiana, or the 501 percent in Alaska, but still an eye-popping rate of interest. It was many times higher than what any formally recognized credit agency would be allowed to charge, and one that left the family literally unable to scratch up enough cash to feed the children properly. They cut down on meat from four nights a week to two, began eating more bread and pasta and less protein, started eliminating fresh fruits and vegetables from their diet. In the summer of 2008, Tammera spent almost every afternoon at Lakeview Park, waiting in line for her children to receive free brown-bagged lunches from a local summer feeding program, then sitting on a blanket on the grass with some friends while the children ate their meals. Without that help, she admitted, the family would have been eating an awful lot of ramen noodles.

■ ■ ■

Interlude II

I shall eat for a few weeks what a million people spend their lives eating, and feel that whatever discomfort it brings me is little enough and willingly taken on, in the scale of all it could take to even us up.

—JAMES AGEE, *Let Us Now Praise Famous Men*

Mother's Day, 2008.

There is a wonderful restaurant in the heart of Old Sacramento that my family dines at on special occasions. It has an old-world ambience, heavy oil paintings on the darkly painted walls, high ceilings, dimly lit chandeliers, and a gorgeous courtyard area for eating brunch. The brick walls of the courtyard are covered with the ivy of elite schools and European castles. It's a good place to politician-watch, as lobbyists and the elected officials they woo tend to patronize the establishment—not least because it has by far the best, and most startlingly expensive, wine list in town. The entrées are somewhere between twenty-five and forty dollars; some of the wine bottles have four figures attached to them.

The Mother's Day brunch is one of my gastronomic hallelujah days. We usually sit at the bar sipping mimosas while we wait for our table. Then, tuxedo-clad waiters usher us downstairs to our seats, presenting my wife and daughter with a red rose each along the way. They bring us steaming coffees, juices for the children, floral-scripted menus.

The first course is always unlimited access to a buffet positively Roman in its extravagance: huge bowls of cut fruit, platters of carefully crafted pastries, cheese bowls, gently baked salmon, vegetables, breads, oven-hot rolls. The second course is a choice of entrées. This particular feast-Sunday, my wife chose a baked seafood frittata; I opted for a filet mignon, cooked rare, with various delicately sculpted vegetable dishes as sides. The meat was thick, but oh-so-delicate, the sort of flesh that a steak knife cuts through like butter. My one-year-old son picked food from our plates; my daughter wallowed in a heaping plate of waffles, cream, and strawberries.

We ate with gusto, returned to the buffet to take extra helpings of fruit and pastries, called our waiters over for more coffee, and then ate some more. They brought us desserts, mouthwatering chocolate mousse, creamy cakes dripped with melted chocolate, the plates decorated with berries. We shoveled the delicious sweets into our mouths, drank yet more cups of coffee. Finally, we had to stop. With the best will in the world, none of us could eat any more.

When the bill came, I got out my credit card and, without a care in the world, signed away over $150. I had just spent, on one meal for the four of us, more than a member of America's new working poor can afford to lay out for a month's worth of food.

Now, it was time to take a deep breath and temporarily embrace exile from the creature comforts with which I have so carefully padded my middle-class, thirty-something life.

The next day, I decided to reinvent myself as a young, single person with no family obligations and little in the way of career opportunities. I appointed myself a figurative McDonald's employee.

The median income for a McDonald's worker nationally was $8.23 per hour in 2008, about standard for the fast-food industry, higher than the earnings of many agricultural workers, home help aides, hotel cleaners, and other rock-bottom jobs. Working forty hours a week for fifty-two weeks a year, that comes to $17,118.40. And

that's a generous estimate, since sick leave and vacations are generally unpaid in low-end service sector jobs. After taxes, in California,
such a worker would take home $14,772 a year. In New York, they'd
end up with slightly less, in many other states a little more. For a
minimum-wage worker earning only the federal minimum in one of
the eighteen states that doesn't have its own higher minimum wage,
a worker would have to cobble together about sixty hours of work a
week, probably at more than one job, to bring in the same amount of
cash. In such circumstances, bringing home more than $15,000 per
year is a virtual impossibility. It's a miniscule amount of money, but,
for a single person, far above the federal poverty threshold. So, no
Medicaid, no access to food stamps.

In my new make-believe role as a McDonald's employee, I am
netting $1,231 a month to live on, assuming the boss doesn't cut my
hours. If I have company health insurance, my monthly contributions will likely be in the $100 range, reducing my take-home pay
to $1,131. (If I don't opt for coverage, the chances are pretty good,
according to researchers at the Census Bureau and Bureau of Labor
Statistics, that over the course of a year I'll spend more on emergency
visits to the doctor and medicines than I would have spent on my
insurance premiums.)

Many fast-food workers work two jobs to make ends meet, but in
a contracting economy the more common story one hears is about
workers losing what hours they have rather than readily being able
to pick up extra ones.

In a relatively affordable city like Fresno, California, say, the average rent for a one-bedroom apartment was $739 a month in 2008. In
Sacramento, where I live, it was $847. And that was more than a year
after the bursting of the housing bubble. Had I been conducting this
experiment two years earlier, my housing costs would have been even
higher. In Los Angeles or San Francisco they still remained high
after the bubble lost its air. Even at the bottom of the market, in the
trailer parks and mobile home communities in the outer 'burbs and

surrounding countryside miles from downtown Sacramento, you'd be hard-pressed to find any sort of living arrangement for less than four hundred dollars a month—and, if you did, your extra commuting costs would more than cancel out the lower rent.

So, I allow myself four hundred dollars for rent; another one hundred dollars for utilities and a modicum of heat on cold evenings—unlike many parts of the country, Sacramento never gets too cold, so heating homes isn't the enormous, potentially crippling cost it is elsewhere; fifty dollars for basic phone service; eighty dollars for payments on an old car; one hundred dollars a month to buy the bare-minimum required insurance for that car; and, given soaring gas prices, one hundred dollars a month to drive to and from work, to the grocery store, and on a few other local errands. For now, I'll assume I'm not carrying a credit card debt and so don't have monthly payments to Visa or Discover Card, and I'll also assume I don't have to pay for a regular prescription refill, or have monthly payments on any furniture or electronic items. There's not much room for error here. I've left myself $301 for household goods, clothes, entertainment, food for the month, miscellaneous unanticipated expenditures, and, hopefully, contributions into my tiny savings account.

I assume I can spend just over half of my $301 on food: about sixty-five to seventy-five dollars every two weeks. That will allow me to buy one or two pairs of jeans a year, perhaps some sneakers and a couple shirts; it will allow me to see a few movies, maybe once in a blue moon catch a baseball game, down some drinks with old friends, spend an evening bowling. But I also keep my credit cards functioning: my intent, like that of most of the people I talked with, is to stay close to my intended budget while not actually going hungry.

Because I have my trusty plastic, I don't shop as I go. On the other hand, because I'm nervous about accumulating debt too quickly, because I worry that my hours will be cut and I won't be able to pay off my bills, that I might need to save my credit card usage for true emergencies, neither do I buy in bulk. I head to Safeway and buy what I hope will be almost enough non-vegetable, non-fruit staples to last two weeks. I'm aiming to keep it to about forty dollars. I buy only on-sale items, canned goods where you can get three for the price of two, a peculiarly cheap box of cereal. I buy a miniscule amount of meat (five slivers of pork loin and a one-and-a-half-pound pack of chicken legs). Two personal-size frozen pizzas. No fresh produce apart from two large, unwashed baking potatoes. My cart has on-sale non–brand name baked beans and pork (the kind with one or two scraps of pork fat in a sea of beans), kidney beans, canned peas, and green beans (again, of the discounted, peculiarly tasteless variety), low-grade sliced bread—the sort you can eat ten slices of and still feel hungry—and six of the cheapest bagels on the shelves. It has two small tubs of fake butter and a small jar of discounted jelly. There are some $1.29 rice cake snacks that I hope I can stretch for two weeks, two jars of on-sale spaghetti sauce, one small box of pasta, a two-pound bag of rice, some low-grade corn oil to cook my wares with, some canned spaghetti rings, two boxes of mac-and-cheese, and the nastiest, cheapest chicken noodle soup in the store. For liquid refreshments, I buy a pint of milk and a quart of sickly-sweet grape-and-cranberry-juice concentrate. I buy on-sale sugar, six eggs, and—to spoil myself—a three-dollar box of brownie mix that I pray will assuage my sweet tooth for fourteen days. (For now, I don't buy coffee and tea, letting myself use up the coffee beans and tea bags that I already have in my house.)

The constriction of choice is stark and immediate. I have encountered the first set of dilemmas faced by the impoverished omnivore: meat, or fruit and vegetables? Starch, or healthy but less filling fare? It's a no-brainer: the filling starch wins out. I have also encountered another reality: nutritional spontaneity is a privilege of affluence; with limited means, every meal has to be carefully planned and calculated in advance.

When I cash out, even with my Safeway's discount card, it's $61.36, far more than I had allotted. That doesn't leave me with much wiggle room. I go to my local farmers market, which, unlike the overpriced organic feel-good markets in New York's Union Square or Los Angeles's Santa Monica, is actually by far the cheapest place in town to buy fresh fruit and vegetables. I purchase a tiny handful of cherries, a one-dollar bag of kiwis, and one orange as my fruit for the two weeks; for vegetables I buy only the cheapest items: three unpeeled carrots, a yam, some spinach, two beets, one onion, and a bunch of radishes. That takes me to the seventy dollar mark. I've already gone over budget.

Eight days in, the remaining slices of my loaf of sliced white bread go moldy and have to be thrown away. I don't buy more since I can just about get by for breakfast on small portions of cereal. I do, though, have to buy another quart of milk, for just over two dollars, when I run out of milk for my bran flakes. I also cheat once and buy just under a quarter pound of low-end ground chuck to mix with my canned kidney beans over a bowl of rice.

My Latte Factor: three small cups of coffee when I'm out of the house for prolonged periods, one glass of cranberry juice in a bar, and, when I start craving doughy food three days after having to throw my bread away, two donuts from the local donut shop. On the second Wednesday, I ponder going to my local McDonald's and indulging in their midweek special: thirty-nine-cent hamburgers. But, given how much I loathe fast food, I decide to hold back on that treat until later in my experiment. I also buy one pint of beer when out with friends.

All told, I've now spent about eighty-five dollars on two weeks worth of food.

I'm by no means starving. In fact, I haven't missed a meal. I have, however, become at least mildly "food insecure." My meals are generally tasteless, deficient in vegetables and fruit, over-reliant on beans, rice, and potatoes. Even though I spend a lot of time thinking up how to cook the food tastefully, realistically all I have at my disposal is food to be eaten in a hurry and forgotten about. My portions are small—which is why my rations last two weeks—and there's not enough for seconds. At mealtimes, I eat every scrap that's on my plate. Had I had twice as much food, I would likely have gone through it in the exact same two weeks. In other words, I'm already stretching my portions to make sure there's enough food for fourteen breakfasts, fourteen lunches, and fourteen dinners. I don't think I've lost weight—though I'm deliberately not keeping track of this information—but by the end of the two weeks I'm already feeling slightly sluggish, just a little under the weather.

I check in with Amy Block Joy, a nutritionist at the University of California at Davis who specializes in food and poverty issues and who has agreed to comment on my diet during the weeks of the experiment. She looks over the list of foods I've consumed and says generally I'm just about staying afloat nutritionally. I do, however, have a vitamin C deficiency, and I'm not putting enough potassium into my body—placing me at risk of heart and kidney problems if I were to maintain this diet over the long term.

I've also become socially invisible. Since I can't afford to visit my local café, I go out far less during the day. And as I'm somewhat embarrassed, even though it's only an experiment, to sit watching while other people eat, I find I'm phoning my friends less often to suggest visits.

By Wednesday of the second week, I'm down to my three cans of spaghetti rings (which I bought only because they were ludicrously cheap, and which, from the picture on the can label, look so starkly unappetizing I hope not to have to open them); a jar of spaghetti sauce, about half a portion of pasta, some soggy radishes and spinach, a can of peas, one egg, two cans of soup, a couple cups of rice, two chicken legs, some leftover baked beans, and one baked potato. I also have a precious square inch left from my baked brownie cake and a rapidly dwindling pile of cheap Kellogg's strawberry bran flakes. I know I'll make it to week's end, but the remainder of the week's going to be something of an endurance test.

And I'm already at least twenty dollars over budget, ten dollars for each week. Were I to do that every week, within a year I'd be five hundred dollars in debt; within two years I'd be one thousand dollars in debt. It doesn't sound like a lot, but for someone working a minimum-wage job, that's a mountainous debt to have to repay. Add in unexpected medical bills, higher gas prices, a couple car tire blowouts, and it doesn't take too long to get a couple thousand dollars in the hole. At that point my minimum monthly credit card payments would start to seriously erode my monthly food budget, and my balancing act would rapidly become impossible. I'd have to put ever more basic purchases on my credit card, and my monthly payments would start spiraling beyond my means to meet. In other words, to avoid going hungry today, I'm making it pretty likely I'll end up going hungry down the road.

By the middle of the two-week cycle, I have discovered a new pastime: scouring the vouchers in the local newspaper, salivating as I look for cheap food deals for my next shopping foray.

THREE

Trickle-up Poverty

Joe worker gets gypped
For no good reason—just gypped.
From the start until the finish comes
they feed him out of garbage cans,
they breed him in the slums.
Joe worker will go
to the shop where stuff is on show.
He'll look at the meat, he'll look at the bread
and too little to eat sort of goes to his head.

—MARC BLITZSTEIN, *The Cradle Will Rock*

DURING THE GREAT DEPRESSION, with a wave of bankruptcies threatening to collapse America's rural economy, the federal government worked both to prop up agricultural prices and to feed the legions of hungry people camped out in cities or roaming the countryside. This was partly because government officials in the Roosevelt administration genuinely believed they had a duty to help America's growing numbers of downtrodden and destitute, to craft innovative institutional responses to an unprecedented economic crisis. Partly, however, it was because they feared the costs of inaction to the social order.

By 1933, when Roosevelt was inaugurated, shantytowns known as Hoovervilles (sarcastically named after Roosevelt's hapless predecessor, Herbert Hoover) had popped up in cities, along riverfronts, and in abandoned railway yards all across America. They housed

America's newly dispossessed, farmers who had been driven off
their land by falling property prices and banks calling in their loans,
urban workers laid off by the owners of shuttered factories in the
years following the 1929 Wall Street crash, young people attempting
to enter a shriveled job market. Their residents cooked on makeshift
outdoor stoves or stood in line at soup kitchens.

A year earlier, tens of thousands of hungry World War I veterans
had marched on Washington, D.C., demanding the government
pay promised military-service bonuses early so that they could feed
their families. The men, known as the Bonus Expeditionary Force,
or, more simply, the Bonus Marchers, staked their tents in open
spaces around the city, occupied several buildings, and held raucous
rallies in support of their claims. "When we got to Washington," a
marcher named Jimmy Sheridan told Studs Terkel, author of the
1970 book *Hard Times*, "there was quite a few ex-servicemen there
before us. There was no arrangements for housing. Most of the men
that had wives and children were living in Hooverville. This was
across the Potomac River—what was known as Anacostia Flats.
They had set up housing there, made of cardboard and of all kinds
[*sic*]." Other marchers, Sheridan recalled, took over vacant buildings
and garages.

The U.S. Senate, unwilling to push the country's already fragile finances further into debt to pay the bonuses, refused to release
money for the hungry veterans. During the summer of 1932, as street
fighting between fascists and communists was intensifying throughout much of Europe, Hoover's government sent saber-wielding, tear
gas–lobbing troops—led by General MacArthur, General Patton,
and Major Eisenhower—into D.C. to clear out the protestors. The
action led to at least one death, dozens of injuries, and the unnerving
spectacle of trained military veterans in open conflict with the government on the streets of the nation's capital. "Thank God," Hoover
was reported to have said. "We still have a government that knows
how to deal with a mob."

In the face of such unrest, for the incoming Roosevelt administration not to have set up programs to alleviate hunger would have been to court disaster. Recent experiences in Germany, where the Nazis were consolidating their hold on power, demonstrated all too vividly that empty bellies could cause entire political systems to fold.

Under the new administration, thousands of destitute veterans were hired, and fed, by the Civilian Conservation Corps (CCC). (Tragically, more than 250 of these CCC-employed Bonus Marchers died in the Florida Keys during a powerful hurricane in 1935.) More generally, government agencies began buying up surplus food from farmers—thus ensuring that prices didn't further collapse—and distributing that food to those too poor to buy it on the open market. Low-income adults could purchase subsidized food stamps from local government agencies. During that period, soup kitchens—catering to the destitute families famously photographed by Dorothea Lange and Walker Evans, and written about by John Steinbeck—could buy food cheaply from the government. And an increasing number of school children (8 million by the end of Roosevelt's presidency) were enrolled in subsidized lunch programs that relied on surplus government-held supplies.

When the Depression gave way to near-full employment during World War II, and after that conflagration left the United States as the world's industrial and agricultural powerhouse, many of the New Deal's welfare programs and public works projects ended. In an age of affluence, organizations such as the Civilian Conservation Corps, or the Tennessee Valley Authority (TVA) were seen as no longer needed. Increasingly, they came to be viewed as hindrances to the smooth functioning of newly confident markets. But a limited food stamp system, one that recipients had to buy into, and a larger school lunch program *did* survive the cuts, and federal farm bills continued to channel billions of dollars in subsidies and guaranteed-purchase agreements to agriculture.

For two decades, from the early 1930s onward, the government had been in the business of feeding at least some of the country's hungry, and, with millions of farmers relying on the Feds to buy up commodities and shore up prices, not much political capital could be gained from stepping away from this commitment. Such government subsidies were, wrote the political scientist Adam Sheingate in his book *The Rise of the Agricultural Welfare State*, a form of state handout premised on the notion of the government assuring mutual benefit for farmers and food consumers alike. Thus a nutritional safety net was woven, one that was largely invisible to the broader public, especially to the middle class, which was moving out of the cities and into large houses in the suburbs, and coming to expect ever more abundance—more income, more food, more space in which to raise the kids. When Lyndon Johnson signed the 1964 Food Stamp Act, designed to make permanent government's role in feeding the hungry, he told his audience in the White House Cabinet Room that "it is one of many sensible and needed steps we have taken to apply the power of America's new abundance to the task of building a better life for every American."

Yet, despite John Kennedy's New Frontier vision, despite Lyndon Johnson's Great Society rhetoric, into the late 1960s the safety net remained small and full of holes. It was better at ensuring regular food supplies for the working poor who could afford to buy into the subsidized food stamp and school lunch program than at providing security to those at the very bottom of the economic ladder. As a result, even after the Food Stamp Act had been signed into law, fewer than 4 million Americans were using the program each month, and in many parts of the country food stamps remained largely unavailable. The same limited scale also held true for school lunches. In historically impoverished regions—the Deep South and Appalachia, in particular, as well as many inner-city ghettoes—an invisible hunger epidemic remained. Far from the media spotlight, malnutrition continued to take a terrible toll on the country's poorest, least noticed communities.

In April 1967, a generation after Franklin Roosevelt pledged to bring America out of its Depression, Senators Robert Kennedy and Joseph Clark visited the Mississippi Delta and interviewed African American residents who were literally starving. The testimony they reaped—the descriptions of malnourished children with bloated bellies, of shacks lacking electricity and with not a whit of food on the shelves—shocked the nation, most of whose residents genuinely believed it had banished hunger from its lands. The senators, author Loretta Schwartz-Nobel wrote in her book, *Starving in the Shadow of Plenty*, "drove along the bleak, unpaved back roads of the Mississippi Delta, stopping at shack after shack and seeing for themselves some of the starving, diseased, and retarded children of America. The men got out of their cars. They put out their hands and touched the children's swollen stomachs. They tried to talk to them but the children were too hungry, too apathetic, or too badly damaged to respond."

Later that year, the Citizens' Board of Inquiry into Hunger and Malnutrition commissioned to review government food programs documented stories of babies dying because their mothers couldn't afford milk for them. It also reported that many hungry people were suffering from such extreme protein and calorie deficiencies that they were coming down with rare diseases such as kwashiorkor and marasmus, symptoms of which included bloated stomachs and faces, severe wasting of body tissue, thinning hair, and flaking, pallid skin. The very exoticism of the names of these diseases hinted at the fact that these were problems not previously thought common to America's shores. One South Carolina doctor reported operating on a young African American girl for appendicitis and discovering her stomach was filled with roundworms. "Of course, in these colored children the closer we get up the ileum in the stomach the more worms we will find, because these kids don't have much to eat. And this is where they head, they get the food before the kids do," the *New York Review of Books* quoted the doctor telling the Board of Inquiry.

Adding fuel to the fire, in May 1968 CBS ran a documentary by the country's most respected television newsman, Edward R. Murrow, titled *CBS Reports: Hunger in America.* The title spoke for itself. Empty bellies were once again big news.

In the wake of Kennedy and Clark's findings, Murrow's reportage, and a series of high-profile follow-up studies carried out by blue ribbon commissions and physicians' task forces, the Johnson and then Nixon administrations massively expanded the country's food stamp program—making it free for the poorest of the poor and near-free for those just above them economically—school breakfast and lunch program, and a subsidy system for senior centers to provide lunches to the elderly. By the mid-1970s, the food stamp system was feeding close to 20 million people, and the school breakfast and lunch program was reaching tens of millions of children.

At the same time, the somewhat chaotic world of charity food centers was streamlined: during the 1970s a national network of food banks, partially reliant on private donations, partially running on USDA-distributed farm surpluses, took root in virtually every major city in America. Their central warehouses served as distribution hubs for smaller food pantries, and the food pantries then doled the food out to hungry clients.

By the end of the decade, while poverty remained endemic in many locales, most experts were optimistic that genuine hunger no longer existed as a major problem in America. In an era that had fallen short of the Johnson administration's proclaimed goal of ending poverty in the United States, the eradication of mass hunger counted as a singular triumph. Through a combination of technical ingenuity—resulting in rising crop productivity, more sophisticated irrigation, new seed technologies and pesticides—and political will,

America had seemingly abolished widespread hunger, making real what many theorists thought to be impossible. It was an achievement comparable in its import to the medical revolutions that had recently eradicated smallpox and largely eliminated polio.

The triumph, however, was short-lived. During the early 1980s, in the first years of Ronald Reagan's presidency, when the Federal Reserve tightened the money supply as a shock-treatment response to galloping inflation, unemployment shot up, as did interest rates. At the same time, the federal government began shrinking social welfare programs and toughening up eligibility requirements for services such as food stamps. Not surprisingly, food pantries and soup kitchens around the country reported an explosive increase in the number of hungry Americans. Food pantries in Boston saw a more than doubling of the number of people needing their help from 1982 to 1984. In Birmingham, Alabama, soup kitchens reported a similar increase in clientele during these years. In Nashville, Tennessee, social services tripled the number of meals given out to indigent elderly people. And in Houston, the food bank increased the amount of food it distributed by more than 700 percent in these same three years. "Hunger has returned to this nation," wrote the authors of the 1985 Physician's Task Force report, *Hunger in America: The Growing Epidemic*, from which the above data was taken. "And all the evidence indicates that it is continuing to grow as a problem."

The decades following have largely been a story of government retrenchment, slice-and-dice operations against state-funded social programs, and the growing neglect—sometimes malign in intent, sometimes simply inept—of America's poor and near-poor residents. The 1994 Contract with America ushered in years of cuts to welfare programs and the introduction of strict time limits for those receiving cash grants such as Temporary Aid to Needy Families (previously known as Aid to Families with Dependent Children). The George W. Bush presidency—eight years that saw the emergence of a yawning income gap between the country's wealthiest and most impoverished residents on a scale not seen since the 1920s—witnessed a further move away from state-funded programs, with many core government obligations toward the poor increasingly farmed out to private, often faith-based charities.

"As Dylan says, 'You don't need to be [*sic*] a weatherman to know which way the wind blows,'" said Joel Berg, executive director of the New York City Coalition Against Hunger. "The lines at food pantries are going through the roof. It's gone from worse to worser. It's horrible grammar, but it really explains what happens: fewer people working, those working, working fewer hours, food prices rising so food stamps buy less, and pantries having less food. So it's a triple whammy."

In New York City, by the summer of 2008 1.1 million residents were on food stamps, and Berg's coalition estimated as many as 700,000 more were eligible but not enrolled in the program. At least in part this was because of the aggressive steps Mayor Rudy Giuliani's administration had taken to kick people off welfare and food stamps a decade earlier. In part, though, this was a national problem. Even as the numbers of people on food stamps rose during the economic crisis that began in 2007, the number of people around the country who were eligible but not receiving aid also increased. By May 2008, more than 28.4 million Americans were receiving food stamps, an increase of 351,000 over the month before, and a rise of more than 2 million from the previous May. At no time in the history of the food stamp program were more Americans receiving this aid. And yet, while almost everyone who was eligible in Missouri, Tennessee, Oregon, and Maine had enrolled—in Oregon's case in response to truly devastating hunger data from a few years earlier—in other states, like California, Colorado, Nevada, and Wyoming, barely half of eligible residents were enrolled. Averaged out across the nation, one in three people who qualified for food stamps—more than 10 million individuals—still weren't receiving them in 2008.

"I think the food stamp system is entirely broken," said Berg. "Any program where 35 to 40 percent of eligible people don't get the benefit is broken." To make up the shortfall, food pantries and soup kitchens were operating in overdrive. With the economy contracting, Berg's organization estimated that 1.3 million residents in New York City and its environs were now eating charity food.

And for the lucky ones who received food stamps, as food inflation hit double digits, their coupons increasingly failed to buy enough groceries to even begin to feed them properly. Texas reported that the declining value of food stamps would effectively deprive the state of nearly $250 million in economic activity in 2009. In the same way as low unemployment no longer guaranteed low levels of poverty, high food stamp enrollments had ceased to indicate that the government was effectively tackling America's escalating hunger crisis.

A single person on food stamps in mid-2008 received an average of twenty-six dollars per week and a maximum of forty dollars in vouchers, far less to meet their basic nutritional needs than most middle-class Americans spent on their largely frivolous Latte Factors. And while a person could survive on twenty-six dollars worth of food each week if they had access to good, cheap, fresh produce stalls and stores like Trader Joe's that sell affordable dairy, cheap eggs, and pasta, they couldn't eat properly on that amount if they were riding public transport and could shop only at local, overpriced corner stores, where shelves are stocked with canned goods and fresh produce is almost nonexistent.

Through mid-2008, elderly food stamp recipients received a derisory ten dollars per month in vouchers in some states. The farm bill, passed in June 2008 over President Bush's veto, raised the minimum, but only up to the still derisory level of fourteen dollars. And to qualify for these vouchers you had to be abysmally poor and willing to go through an array of bureaucratic humiliation rituals. In many parts of the country, the food stamp application paperwork now stretches to dozens of pages; and recipients in many states have to fill out this paperwork again every month or two to prove their ongoing eligibility, an extraordinarily time-consuming and humiliating means test for people already on the financial edge. All states have at least some asset caps in place, meaning people who own houses or relatively new cars are largely ineligible for food stamps—even if they are cash poor, have recently lost their jobs, had health-care emergencies, or have run up heating bills they cannot pay during the cold months of winter.

Not surprisingly, there is a huge and growing pool of hungry people who either don't qualify or don't bother to apply for such aid. Some of them fall back on food banks; others try to tough out the hard times on their own.

In Amarillo, Zack Wilson recalled the story of one lonely elderly widow. She lived in the tiny Panhandle community of Tulia, and her only companion was a cat. Unable to afford food both for herself and for her pet, she chose to buy cat food. When the workers from a mobile food pantry unit visited her, "her cupboards were literally empty apart from cat food. To survive, she was eating cat food," Wilson explained. "She would, through family members or whatnot, receive money. But she chose to take care of her pet first. If you're elderly, you turn to your pet for companionship. And that's what she was eating to survive."

During the Clinton presidency, Joel Berg worked in the Department of Agriculture, setting up a small Food Recovery and Gleaning Initiative to make sure donated food was effectively distributed to where it was needed most. He also got permission to start work on a Community Food Security Initiative, intended to broaden access to healthy foods in poor neighborhoods through the creation of community gardens, local farmers markets with the ability to accept food stamps, and other innovative proposals. When George W. Bush was elected in November 2000, Berg sent the incoming administration several long memos explaining these new initiatives. He never heard back from them. In January 2001, the new programs were shut down.

"I didn't think things were going to be good," Berg recollected eight years later, sitting in his tiny third-floor office in lower Manhattan, three blocks south of Wall Street, one wall dominated by photos of Berg with the Clintons, another wall bedecked with African masks, a third showing a restaurant sign reading "Eat, or We Both Starve." "I just didn't know how un-good it was going to be."

Things got a little better for antihunger workers following passage of the 2008 farm bill. Among its many multibillion-dollar provisions, the bill partially shored up USDA donations to food banks, raised USDA commodity spending $140 million to $250 million annually, and indexed the amount for inflation. Yet, for many food bank workers, it was too little, too late. From 2002 through 2007, as the global food market tightened up, domestic surpluses declined, and much of the remaining surplus got snapped up to feed soldiers fighting in Iraq and Afghanistan, charity food networks got hammered. The amount of USDA food provided to California's food banks declined from 97 million pounds to 39 million pounds per year. The California Association of Food Banks estimated that the 2008 farm bill would add 12 million pounds of food, leaving USDA contributions still far short of the 2002 levels, while the numbers of people needing food help continued to soar.

Similar stories of collapsing USDA contributions to food banks during the Bush years could be heard around the country. In a Washington dominated by conservative ideologues, the will did not exist to halt the slide into hunger for tens of millions of Americans. In this funhouse inversion of reality, Robert Rector, senior research fellow at the Heritage Foundation—the Republican Party's favorite think tank—could, in all seriousness, claim that poor people's poor diets were exclusively a matter of bad choices rather than lack of money and access to healthy food. "Most adults in food insecure households actually consume too much, not too little, food," Rector wrote in November 2007. "Contrary to the claims of poverty advocates, the major dietary problem facing poor Americans is too much, not too little, food. Public policies should be directed toward encouraging the poor to avoid chronic over-consumption, exercise more, and reduce intake of foods rich in fat and added sugar."

Why the government, along with conservative policy research institutes, failed for so long to consider so many clearly poor Americans as living in poverty, and why it neglected to act to restore dignity to these broken—or breaking—lives, is a sorry story of conservative economic analysis meeting conservative politics, of ideology serving as a blinder to the facts on the ground.

One of the key measures of an economy's health is its inflation rate, a measure somewhat analogous to blood pressure readings at the doctor's office: you want to have some limited degree of inflation because that generally is a sign of economic growth. No blood pressure, no life; no price movements, no economic dynamism. But you don't want too much inflation, because that shows your economy's fundamentals are out of whack and, like high blood pressure, puts you at risk of suffering a whole bunch of nasty consequences. Since the years of stagflation in the 1970s and early 1980s, when the global economy was beset by high inflation, low economic growth, and high unemployment, economic policy makers have made controlling inflation a priority. Countries, or economic blocs, set themselves inflation targets, and government spending and lending patterns are then modified to meet these goals. When poorer countries have failed to control inflation themselves, organizations such as the International Monetary Fund (IMF) or the World Bank have threatened to pull their loans. Such threats force implementation of "structural readjustment" policies, which generally involve cuts in government social spending, as the price of continuing to do business on the world stage.

Wealthy countries, such as the United States, have developed complex measurement instruments to gauge their own inflation levels. They survey large numbers of businesses to find out what wholesale inflation runs to, and even larger numbers of households and retailers to track the inflation rate that is passed on to consumers. The government tracks inflation in specific sectors of the economy, such as wage inflation, price inflation, and many other subcategories. The most widely quoted number, however, is the one referred to as the Consumer Price Index (CPI), a detailed estimate of how consumer prices change month by month, based around a weighted basket of goods. If, for example, an average urban household spends 5 percent of their income on telecommunications, prices related to that area of the economy will be given a "weight" to reflect that one in every twenty household dollars goes there. If clothing represents, say, 2 percent, then prices in the clothing sector will be weighted to reflect that only one in fifty household dollars goes that way. Weight enough goods and then track their price changes over the months of a year, and a fairly accurate inflation index becomes possible.

Historically, however, some areas of the economy have experienced far more price volatility than others. The chief culprits here are food and energy. As a result, the CPI, which is designed to show durable trends over time, doesn't include month-by-month price changes in these arenas. Then there's health care, which has been soaring in cost over the past decade. However, because the technology has been changing so rapidly, comparing the costs of health insurance today to that of ten or twenty years ago is in many ways to compare apples and oranges—if you're insured, the dollars you are spending are buying access to a whole lot more services than were available a few years ago. So economists do a fudge here by including some out-of-pocket health-care costs in inflation estimates but excluding the cost of insurance premiums.

A similar tap dance is done around products such as cars, computers, and cell phones. Because the quality of these goods has improved so rapidly in recent years, the CPI contains various "quality adjustment" and "substitution" equations that try to factor in technological progress as a part of the price calculation. As a result, in some cases increases in sticker price for consumers can actually show up as decreases on the CPI charts, if increased computer memory or car performance levels are deemed to more than neutralize the price rise.

Finally, there's housing costs. In the decades leading up to the 2007 housing bust, the cost of buying a house soared, in many areas of the country by several hundred percent. But, that wasn't just a cost; when you buy a house you're also creating a financial asset for yourself. And so economists looking at inflation came up with another way of measuring housing costs. Instead of simply inputting the cost of a mortgage, they tried to work out how much of an increase there would be from one year to the next for the equivalent rental cost of the owner-occupied home. And that entirely fictitious dollar amount was what got keyed into the CPI equation.

Because of all these exclusions and modifications, you might be spending vastly more on the key items in your life—food, health care, energy, housing—than you were a year or two earlier, yet the CPI numbers will still tell you that inflation is only running to 3 or 4 percent a year. That was particularly true from 2005 to mid-2008, when energy prices were rising up into the stratosphere.

But surely numbers don't mislead, right? Wrong.

It is tempting to think of economics as a pure science, and the calculation of inflation as akin to a lab experiment or a series of high-resolution photographic images. In fact, it's more akin to impressionism than science. Usually, the picture produced is fairly representative of the broader landscape, but it certainly isn't a pure reproduction. If you are a middle-class suburbanite in middle America, the consumer price index probably captures annual changes in your out-of-pocket expenditures pretty well. It's less good at distinguishing geographic disparities—soaring housing costs in

New York or California, say, or rising food costs in Hurricane-hit areas of the Gulf Coast, or state-specific spikes in gas or electricity costs. And things get even weirder when the CPI is used to calculate changes in needs for the urban poor or for rural Americans from one year to the next. *Why?* Because the basket of goods used to estimate inflation isn't indicative of how poor and rural Americans spend their money. Poor people tend to spend far more of their income on food, health care, gas, and utilities than do their middle-class neighbors; and those are precisely the items whose prices went up fastest for much of the Bush presidency. They are also, in the short term, the items least accurately factored into inflation estimates by government economists.

"Changes in energy and food are going to impact the poor much more," believed Mary Kokoski, a Bureau of Labor Statistics (BLS) economist who, since the mid-1990s, had been looking at the possibility of developing a separate Consumer Price Index (CPI) for poor Americans. In the 1990s, when food and energy prices were low and relatively stable, Kokoski and her colleagues didn't find significant differences in inflation rates for poor and middle-class consumers. In 2007 and 2008, however, the economic conditions would likely have produced very disparate results for these different income groups. *So why hadn't the BLS moved ahead with the new CPI calculations?* Because of years of budget cuts. "So," said Kokoski, "we haven't been able to collect the supplemental data we'd need."

"It's not a priority," Bob Pollin explained in frustration. "It wouldn't be hard to do. But addressing the needs of the working poor is not a priority."

All of these inflation-estimate fudges allow the government to keep the poverty line—which is tied to the official inflation rate—artificially low, and the level of government benefits, also tied to inflation, correspondingly low. In real life, this situation erodes the value of those benefits and limits the numbers of Americans who qualify for such state-funded aid in the first place. The end results fit perfectly with the low-tax, downsize-government rhetoric that conservatives have run with. (Witness the infamous comment by Grover Norquist, president of Americans for Tax Reform, that he'd like to shrink government down to the size where it could be strangled in the bathtub.) Liberals have begrudgingly lived with this approach for most of the past four decades. Create a convenient fiction within which there is less apparent need for government services and it suddenly becomes a whole lot easier to corrode the quality and breadth of those services.

Ronald Reagan defended tax cuts for wealthy Americans by referring to a "trickle-down effect," by which money freed up at the top of the economic chain seeped into the broader economy, creating a domino effect of spreading affluence. In hindsight, however, the legacy of his conservative economics involves at least as much an adverse "trickle-up effect," by which inadequate government aid programs, limited by underestimations of inflation and legislative fiat, created a pool of peculiarly vulnerable people at the bottom of the economy. These men and women were, for all intents and purposes, forced to work minimum-wage jobs; and the minimum wage, in its turn, was then effectively stripped of its value by inflation and a decade-long effort by Republicans in Congress to block all moves to raise its dollar value. This, then, meant that employers offering jobs at just above minimum-wage rates could keep their wages down. And thus, the pain crept up the economic ladder, eating away at the financial security of tens of millions of people.

As the economy tanked in 2008, cities like Reno, Fresno, Seattle, Chattanooga, and Columbus all began reporting stunning increases in the size of their local homeless populations. People who had recently owned homes and then lost them, or who had lost their jobs and been evicted from homes they could no longer pay the rent on, were, like the Hooverville residents of the post-1929 years, forced to live out of residential hotels. When these filled up, residents moved on, sleeping in their cars or in shantytowns that the media dubbed "tent cities." Located on abandoned railway yards, undeveloped lots, and scrublands, many of these improvised communities, whose tightly packed rows of small tents gave them the appearance of refugee camps on the edge of war zones, came to house hundreds of people.

The families would bring their meager possessions with them, bags and suitcases piled up inside the tents. For food, many of them would line up at soup kitchens and pantries, long lines of misery snaking through the down-at-heel parts of town.

In the upscale beach town of Santa Barbara, California, local officials opened up city car parks at night for homeless families to park and sleep in their vehicles. Outside Los Angeles, one tent city resident told BBC reporters in March 2008 that he had had to choose between "feeding my family or keeping the house." And so, the reporters drily noted, the tent-dwelling man explained that, "I got rid of the house."

With the poor getting poorer, and more people becoming poor, it shouldn't have surprised anybody when *New York Times* reporter Larry Bartels wrote, in an April 27, 2008, article, that 80 percent of all net income gains in America in the years since Ronald Reagan's election had gone to the top 1 percent of income earners, "boosting their share of total income to levels unseen since before the Great Depression."

The final piece of the puzzle here involves another convenient fiction. Underestimating inflation allows the Federal Reserve to keep interest rates artificially low, which is good for economic growth. Low interest rates facilitate—or did until the credit freeze of the late summer and autumn of 2008—the flow of money from banks to consumers, homebuilders, retail businesses, and so on. Such low rates, however, may well have contributed to the massive and unsustainable run-up in home prices in the 1990s and early 2000s, and the extraordinary expansion of mortgage lending to financially under-qualified borrowers. A plus for the economy in the short term—for it encouraged more and more Americans to borrow to pay for more and more consumption—these trends eventually set the housing market up for the collapse that began in 2006 and continued, three years later, to send hundreds of thousands of homeowners into default and then foreclosure, and to cause cascading bank and insurance failures throughout much of the world.

In a very real sense, many of the victims of the foreclosure epidemic are pawns in a much larger game of casino capitalism, one in which wealth is generated not so much by the production of goods as by the continual, and increasingly opaque, shuffling of debt. As America's manufacturing base declined from the 1970s onward, liberal and conservative administrations alike bought into this practice. One of the most important pieces of legislation that deregulated banking and investment systems happened during Bill Clinton's presidency when, in 1999, the Financial Services Modernization Act was passed. This act allowed individual companies to serve as bankers, mortgage brokers, investment middlemen, and insurers, paving the way for a huge expansion in the number and value of loans issued. A few years later, with George Bush as president, the Federal Reserve pushed down overnight interest rates to 1 percent, dangerously overstimulating the lending markets and further reshaping the American economy as an animal feeding off finances rather than manufacturing.

Consumers mold their choices and spending patterns in response to signals sent by the government and other large institutions. Send enough signals that borrowing is a social good, one that comes with very low costs attached, and, no surprise, you end up with a pervasive culture of reckless spending. Like any other Ponzi scheme, this works for as long as everyone's willing to play the game; it fails, and fails hard, as soon as people start getting nervous and begin calling in their loans.

"Between 1987 and 2007," political commentator Kevin Phillips wrote in his 2008 book *Bad Money*, "debt—in all flavors, from credit card and mortgage to staid U.S. treasury and exotic Wall Street—became one of the nation's largest, fastest-growing businesses. Over those two decades, so-called credit market debt roughly quadrupled from nearly $11 trillion to $48 trillion." With considerable prescience, Phillips argued that "the great bubble blown up over a quarter century is starting to quiver and leak. These are not circumstances in which a nation should put faith in an overgrown and overextended financial services sector, with its bankrupt mortgage lenders, hotshot hedge funds, and reckless megabanks."

Maybe not. But for three decades, doing so had at least partially obscured a growing rot at America's economic core and provided plausible cover for successive governments to hide the scale of poverty and need in America.

Reducing the government's commitment to feeding the poor and providing them with a financial cushion, in part by deliberately underestimating the extent of poverty in the United States, is one component of a generational rollback of the social safety net; it is both a cause and a symptom of the reemergence of divisions in American economic life not seen since before the New Deal. While there isn't wholesale starvation in modern-day America, there *is* now a vast amount of chronic hunger, the sort that leaves a person alive but lethargic, able to work but prone to sickness, depression, and rage. The reemergence of breadline U.S.A. is, in many ways, the ultimate measure of how, over the course of a generation, a political and economic realignment, bookended by Reagan's "smiling conservatism" and Bush's "compassionate conservatism" failed to protect the nation's poor.

Quite simply, for three decades America turned its back on a growing hunger epidemic, allowed the advances of the 1960s and 1970s to be rolled back in pursuit of some sort of ideological market purity, and relied on an inadequate network of private charities and food banks to fill the gap in government services. The result: a level of hunger reminiscent of the 1930s, but without the iconic imagery provided by chroniclers like James Agee, Walker Evans, Dorothea Lange, and John Steinbeck, who cast a cultural spotlight on the poverty. Hunger in modern-day America became, thus, a behind-closed-doors, out-of-sight-out-of-mind catastrophe.

As a result of the economic and political drift, many millions of Americans have ended up on hunger lines. The problem affects not only the homeless and vagrant but increasingly workers employed by small private companies, large corporations, and even the biggest employer in the country: the federal government.

Like the hungry Bonus Marchers from 1932, many of today's hungry are military personnel and their families, living on starting salaries for enlisted men of barely $16,000 per year. In 1991, close to twenty thousand men and women in uniform were on food stamps. That number declined in the 1990s, but in 1999, as Bill Clinton's presidency wound down and presidential hopefuls jockeyed for primary season advantages, Senator John McCain informed his Senate colleagues that eleven thousand active duty personnel and their families remained poor enough to have enrolled on food stamps. Tens of thousands more were turning to private charities for help. "We must end the days of a 'food-stamp Army' once and for all," the Vietnam veteran told his colleagues. It didn't happen. Five years later, journalist Barbara Ehrenreich reported in *The Progressive* magazine that the families of twenty-five thousand military personnel were poor enough to qualify for food stamps. And in the years since the wars in Afghanistan and Iraq began, food pantries near army bases in states from California to Georgia have reported startling jumps in demand for their services. Others have had to ramp up their operations to help out the families of reservists and National Guardsmen, called away from their civilian jobs and repeatedly sent overseas on multiple tours of duty.

In February 2008, Helene Meissner, director of the Northwest

New Jersey Community Action Program's food bank, recalled, "Some people came to us and told us that in the beginning of June there were going to be more than three thousand New Jersey National Guardsmen deployed, and they asked us if it was possible to set up an emergency food pantry for their families. Some of them, when the head of the household goes off to war, their income is depleted by in some cases 80 percent. That has a huge impact."

The food bank agreed to set up two pantries, one in the town of Port Murray, the other in a room inside the Phillipsburg armory, exclusively for the families of military personnel. Local churches donated food, as did Phillipsburg's Masonic lodge, the local police department, and area schools. By the end of the summer, the organizers estimated, over two hundred local families were receiving free food boxes.

"They're all my past students," onetime high school principal and U.S. Navy veteran Bill Nixon said of the young New Jersey National Guardsmen, explaining why he was working so hard to find food for their families. "They've been out of high school maybe two years. They're young and have young families. Maybe one-third of them are married. A couple of them, their wives were pregnant when they left. It probably wasn't expected by many of them they'd be activated and sent to Iraq for nine months. Most thought they'd be stateside. Most of them took a pay cut of more than half. It's a huge cut in their annual income. So the purpose of the food drive is to help supplement the families, to help take care of them while their loved ones are gone."

■ ■ ■

Interlude III

He was so weary after a whole month of
concentrated wretchedness and gloomy
excitement that he longed to rest, if only
for a moment, in some other world, whatever
it might be; and, in spite of the filthiness of
the surroundings, he was glad now to stay
in the tavern.

—FYODOR DOSTOYEVSKY, *Crime and Punishment*

When I began my experiment, I had assumed that I would be able
to go through several two-week pay cycle permutations in which I
progressively tightened the screws on a hypothetical working poor
person, while remaining above the food stamp–defined nutritional
safety net. The food stamp program, available to people whose income is no more than 130 percent of the official poverty level, gives
an average of $26 per week per person in food vouchers, and a maxi-
mum of $162 in any given month—and it only gives that top amount
to extremely poor people. Many seniors, in particular, qualify only
for the bare minimum: $14 a month. The idea here is that they still
have some assets left to sell off or deplete—cars above a token resale
value, more than $3,000 in cash assets—before qualifying as totally
destitute. Food stamp architects assume that pretty much anyone
with even a bare minimum of paid income is going to be enough
above the poverty threshold to be able to spend at least that much on
food and thus not need state help.

So, my starting premise was that a fair number of things would have to go wrong, and I would probably have to add in a fair degree of fiscal irresponsibility on my part, before I'd fall beneath the rather meager government-defined food safety net.

Instead, I found that the first time I added in one all-too-realistic financial change, my forty-hour per week, $8.23 per hour, $400 per month in rent alter-ego worker hit the skids. To buy enough food, I would have to go further into debt, thus beginning a cycle that would rapidly make my monthly minimum credit card payments impossible to maintain without further eroding my already min-iscule spending power. Alternately, I could start letting my utility bills, car payments, or even mortgage or rent obligations slide.

Weeks one and two had been relatively easy: a mild credit card crutch ensured that my diet was sufficient if not luxurious; and I kept myself nourished without going into the sort of debt that would immediately cripple me. But then I added ten dollars a week in gas money—which is a conservative estimate, given what happened to gas prices in the first half of 2008. Many workers I spoke with dur-ing my research were spending twenty or thirty dollars more per week on gas by mid-2008 than a year earlier. Those extra few dollars to fill my car took me from about seventy dollars every two weeks for food down to fifty dollars, already two dollars below the average food stamp threshold and fully thirty dollars below the maximum food stamp allotment for a single person.

There were still a couple cups worth of rice left over from the ear-lier weeks, enough fake butter and corn oil for at least several days, the spaghetti rings, and one can of soup. I considered these my nest egg for a rainy day, and, with that cheery thought, went shopping.

While I hadn't had any fish or any meat worth the name for several weeks, what I was really missing was fresh produce. It was the texture of pulpy fruit—the juice bursting out of a segment of orange, the crisp skin of a grape giving way to my teeth—that had me salivating after my meager helpings of food were gone for the day. So I spent about three dollars on a few bananas, three small oranges, and one apple. I also forked over a couple dollars on small portions of fresh vegetables—a cucumber, two yams, one potato, a large onion, a small bag of carrots, eleven little mushrooms, and one tiny yellow squash—enough for a few slivers of vegetables with each of my evening meals over the two weeks to come. And a few more dollars on beans and tortillas. These goodies were only remotely affordable because I happened to drive past a cheap roadside stall off the highway one day. My total expenditures for this food came to $11.10. Were I without a car or unable to pay for gas, that would not have been an option.

In fact, later, when I tried to replicate my shopping expedition in an inner-city corner store in Sacramento's Oak Park district, less than a mile from the city's largest food bank, instead of $11.10 my little basket of food came to $18.75. And none of it was fresh—*yes, the owner said, sometimes he had bananas and other fresh fruit, just not right at the moment.* And so, instead of bananas, oranges, and an apple, I bought a small jar of apple sauce, a can of fruit cocktail mix, and another of sliced pineapples. Instead of fresh yams and potatoes, I ended up with a dented can of yams and a box of mashed potato mix. For my vegetables, I took a small can of mushrooms, two cans of corn, and one mixed vegetable can. The only two things I managed to exactly duplicate from the roadside stall were the can of beans and the package of tortillas.

Yet, despite the rock-bottom prices I paid at the roadside stand, the fruit and vegetables I bought meant that I couldn't afford fruit juice; instead, I bought a one-dollar liter bottle of discounted iced tea to last the two weeks. Even without my pizza and brownies, I still couldn't spring for more than a smidgen of meat: one pound of the lowest quality ground chuck to last the entire two weeks, and ten on-sale frozen sausage links (which, when I heated them up, I discovered were on sale for a reason: they were dried, shriveled little things, light years removed from being recognizably meat). I divided the meat into small bags, kept them in the freezer until they were needed, and sprinkled tiny portions of the fatty ground chuck onto my endless plates of rice and beans. I saved my dozen eggs for dinners, and ate bread or cheap yogurt with sliced bananas for breakfasts. I started skipping lunch, or just eating one potato as my midday meal—and, almost without my being aware of it, I began moving my dinner hour forward. At the start of the cycle, I was eating dinner at seven o'clock; by the end, I'd be ready for food by five thirty. For dessert I'd cram fistfuls of chocolate animal crackers into my mouth—I had found a tub of them on sale for two dollars and change.

Like so many low-income workers hit particularly hard by rising gas prices—self-employed truckers and salesmen, for example—for three days during these two weeks I was on the road. While breakfasts came with the motel room, I had no choice but to buy fast-food meals for lunches and dinners. Over three days, during which I interviewed farmworkers in California's Central Valley, I spent fifteen dollars. Then, bored beyond endurance by my Spartan living arrangements, I went out for drinks with a friend one night; the two beers I bought, my one extravagance during the fourteen-day period, further torpedoed my budget.

When I ran out of milk one week in, I spent fifty-five cents on a half-pint carton. It was enough for my morning coffee, but it meant from then on my cereal bowls would be dry. The bread and tortillas disappeared. The fruits and vegetables ran out. Halfway through, I spent another four dollars replenishing them. I bought two small cups of coffee from cafés and a couple donuts from a drive-up stand. When I cooked meals, I started halving the size of my portions. My plates were so empty after each meal I could almost have put them straight back into the cupboards. The only two meals I ate until I was full during those two weeks were barbeques my family was invited to by friends.

Two days before my two-week cycle ended, I was down to one potato, two small carrots, one orange, a few licks worth of fake butter, the bottom of my bottle of corn oil, a tiny yellow squash, a few handfuls of Trader Joe's Honey Nut O's, perhaps a half serving of cheap, terrible-tasting pasta, and my rainy day stash: one can of soup and three cans of spaghetti rings.

With the exception of the two beers, I had shopped and eaten as intelligently and cheaply as I possibly could, heeding the advice of my University of California at Davis nutritionist on how to make my money go far. I had given myself access to the sort of good, affordable fruits and vegetables that, in reality, most poor people do not have available to them. And yet, despite my best efforts, I had still spent somewhere in the region of seventy dollars and come perilously close to running my food supply down to nothing. And even then, I had only managed to eke out the days by going further into a cycle of credit card debt.

FOUR

Big-Box Special

Hunger makes a human being lapse into a state of
lethargy, especially city hunger. Is there any place
else in the world where a human being is supposed
to go hungry amidst plenty without an outcry,
without protest, where only the boldest steal
or kill for bread, and the timid crawl the streets,
hunger like the beak of a terrible bird at night?
—MERIDEL LE SUEUR, *Women on the Breadlines* (1932)

THERE ARE A LOT OF PEOPLE in the United States military, but even
more people work for Wal-Mart. These days, 1.3 million Americans,
close to 1 percent of the country's workforce, are employed by the behemoth. Globally, 2 million men and women—nearly one in every
three thousand humans alive today—are directly employed by the
company, with millions more dependent on the income brought in
by these workers or by people working for companies that supply
Wal-Mart with goods to sell.

As recently as 1979, Wal-Mart's annual sales were a mere $1 bil-
lion. Throughout the 1980s, Wal-Mart was still just one among many
large-scale clothing and food stores competing for the nation's business. Then Wal-Mart began a relentless march into the big leagues.
By 1997, its annual revenues topped $100 billion. And a decade later,
it was listed by Fortune 500 as being America's largest company,
with annual revenues of over $378 billion. Its profits had soared to

nearly $13 billion. If Wal-Mart were a country, it would have had the world's twenty-fifth largest gross domestic product (GDP), ranking just behind Saudi Arabia and just above Austria. Its profits alone outstripped the GDP of countries such as Honduras, Paraguay, Armenia, Nepal, and the vast, but poorly developed, Democratic Republic of the Congo.

Wal-Mart's gigantic scale alone isn't necessarily a problem. What ultimately makes the company so poisonous is the way it has achieved its success. From the get-go, Wal-Mart has paid low wages, opposed unionization efforts among its workers, and bought labor peace by providing workers with discounted stock—which is all well and good during bull markets, when workers can at least feel like they have a paper cushion, but doesn't help employees pay their bills during bear times. The Wal-Mart model contains a series of race-to-the-bottom feedback loops. Having reached a critical mass, it now uses its scale to force down the rates charged by its suppliers, allowing it to keep its sticker prices lower than those of its competitors. As more rivals are driven out of business, suppliers' options to sell their goods elsewhere decrease, locking them into an increasingly lopsided relationship with Wal-Mart. A similar story holds with wages and benefits. Wal-Mart pays lower wages and offers fewer benefits than many of its retail competitors. In 2008 the corporation estimated its average hourly wage was $10.83. Opponents contend it's even lower. Wal-Mart Watch, an organization set up by labor advocates to monitor Wal-Mart practices in the United States and overseas, claims the starting pay for most workers is between seven and eight dollars. Many employees who have worked for Wal-Mart for more than five years still earn less than ten dollars per hour, putting them below the living-wage threshold identified by economists such as Bob Pollin.

Moreover, Wal-Mart employees have to pay huge out-of-pocket health insurance contributions, deductibles, and co-pays, in some cases over 40 percent of the total cost of the insurance. As a result, a far lower percentage of the company's employees access the available health plans than is the case for other retail chains such as Costco and Target. In 2005, *Dollars and Sense* magazine calculated that only 41 to 46 percent of Wal-Mart's employees had signed up for company-provided health insurance.

So why don't employees simply up and move to work for other stores? For the simple reason that the competitors can't compete with Wal-Mart on prices, and so, while Wal-Mart expands, many other chains stagnate, contract, or go out of business. They no longer have the market clout to employ more workers. And so, like the suppliers, the workers are also increasingly lumped with Wal-Mart—or with copycat chains who realize their best chance of surviving in a *mano a mano* with the mega-company is by adopting the tactics and employment model of their competitor. When Wal-Mart geared up to open forty superstores around California, the unionized grocery store companies Ralphs, Vons, and Albertsons demanded a two-year pay freeze and greater health insurance contributions from their employees, as well as the right to pay new staff lower wages. Seventy thousand supermarket workers went on strike, but the companies stuck to their demands; after several months the strikers returned to work defeated. From then on, supermarket workers in California would no longer receive the middle-class wages and benefits that their unions had fought for, and won, over the course of decades.

Why did the California stores play such a hardball game and risk massive worker discontent? Probably because Wal-Mart's growing presence had bankrupted more than two dozen national supermarket chains since the early 1990s, and the California trio feared they would be next in line to go. In many parts of the country, Wal-Mart had essentially cornered the market on the sale of food, clothing, pharmaceuticals, and household products. "Other companies pay low wages," argued Stacie Locke Temple, Wal-Mart Watch's senior director for strategy and communications. "But the reason we focus on Wal-Mart and the reason it is so critical is it is so large they really do drive what is competitive in terms of benefits and wages. They have a tremendous impact in determining what market wages are in an area and driving down [those] market wages."

On the surface, this is all good for consumers; after all, it results in lower prices. "Always low prices," was Wal-Mart's reassuring advertising jingle from 1988 through September 2007. Then the company updated its slogan to the even more seductive, "Save Money. Live Better." Its handsomely paid executives routinely portray themselves as virtual working-class heroes, crusaders for the little man under assault from elitist critics. The store's determination to undercut the prices charged by competitors was necessary, ex-CEO Lee Scott argued, because fully one in five Wal-Mart customers didn't have checking accounts and needed access to ultra-cheap goods.

But, like most things too good to be true, there's a rub. Increasingly Wal-Mart's shoppers, and the shoppers at look-alike stores, are also Wal-Mart's employees, or workers at the look-alikes. Which leads to a couple questions: Do the low prices paid by people wearing their consumer hats make up for the low wages, the poor health-care benefits, and the negligible retirement plans they receive when wearing their worker hats? Do the cheap blue jeans and rock-bottom DVDs make up for the fact that many Wal-Mart workers have to fall back on state heating assistance programs, food stamps, WIC, state-provided health care for children, and even Medicaid? In Georgia, in 2005, one in four Wal-Mart employees had enrolled their children in the state-funded PeachCare health-care system. In D.C., staffers for Democrats on the House Committee on Education and the Workforce calculated that a single two-hundred-employee Wal-Mart store cost taxpayers over $400,000 per year in public services provided to the underpaid workers. A 2004 report by researchers at the University of California at Berkeley's Institute of Industrial Relations and Center for Labor Research and Education (since renamed the Institute for Research on Labor and Employment) estimated that Wal-Mart workers in California were using $86 million a year worth of public assistance. Similar research has been carried out in many other states by the AFL-CIO, the country's largest trade union federation.

For fifty-seven-year-old Aubretia Edick, a longtime Wal-Mart employee in the depressed upstate New York community of Hudson, the answer to these questions was a resounding *No*. Aubretia, a diminutive lady with short, dull-brown hair, and a kindly, crooked-toothed smile, had been employed at the superstore since 2001, taking the job shortly after she divorced her longtime husband and moved from New York City to the town her elderly stepfather lived in. Her mother had died; her stepfather, a retired machinist, was at a loose end. To fill his days, he worked in the local Wal-Mart as a maintenance man. It was through him that Aubretia got her job. (A few years later, he had a stroke while at work, and instead of calling an ambulance the manager called Aubretia to take him home. The stroke left him paralyzed and unable to live alone.)

When Aubretia began work in the lawn and garden department at the store in 2001, she earned $6.40 an hour. Seven years later, she was earning $10.50. It was a scandalously low wage, but there was nowhere else to go. Factor in inflation, and Aubretia's take home pay wasn't much higher than when she first started. Moreover, even though she was listed as a full-time employee, her manager often cut her hours. Many weeks, she worked as little as twenty-five hours. Hardly ever did she snag more than thirty-five. During one two-week pay period in mid-2008, she made $572.84. Subtract taxes, Social Security, health and dental insurance premiums, and the ten dollars employees were "encouraged" to use to buy Wal-Mart stock every two weeks, and Aubrey was left with $390.37 for fifty-one hours and eighteen minutes of work. Some weeks she earned less; some weeks a little more. Every few months the store added in a few hundred dollars of "bonus" money to generate a bit of good cheer among the underpaid staff.

Aubretia drove a white Oldsmobile Alero, which she had managed to pay off over several years in $157 monthly payments. It cost her eighty dollars a month to insure. She put as little gas into the Alero as possible, and yet as prices spiked she found herself spending more than twenty dollars a week just to drive the few miles a day to work and back and to visit her sick stepdad. When money was really tight, she would sometimes walk the two or three miles each way to work to save a few dimes on gas. She had to pay for her phone and Internet service, visits to the doctor—her insurance came with a one thousand dollar deductible, rendering it little better than catastrophic coverage—as well as for medicines (twenty dollars copay per prescription even after the deductible was spent down) for a thyroid problem, chronic anxiety, and osteoporosis.

She had a small amount of credit card debt, part of which was the result of a Wal-Mart marketing ploy. A couple years earlier, the company had offered employees at her store Wal-Mart credit cards, with no interest attached for the first year so long as they spent $250 the day they signed up for the card. It had sounded like a good deal; so now Aubretia had a flat screen monitor for her computer along with a credit card bill that, while reasonably small, she still couldn't quite pay off.

She lived in a tiny apartment with a nonworking stove and a fridge that barely kept cold what little food she had. Her rent ran to $350 a month; the utilities, even with $300 a year in low-income energy assistance grants, to about $100 a month. And to keep the bills even to that level in the bitter New England winter, she had to let her apartment cool off to not much more than fifty degrees. Now, even when it wasn't cold, Aubrey would catch herself shivering. As for her Latte Factor, it was a paltry forty cents a day—for one soda, which she made last for hours, that had enough caffeine, combined with that from many cups of tea, to give her enough oomph to get through her shift.

But the numbers still didn't compute. Add up all her necessary expenses, and she had literally no possibility of balancing her budget.

So Aubretia, like many of her colleagues, had to skimp on food. Some weeks she'd barely spend more than ten dollars on feeding herself. "I buy my food as I need it. I don't eat that much. I'll take a sandwich to work and that's about it. I drink a lot of tea. Once in a blue moon I'll go into Save-A-Lot and I'll get some meat. I like rice. I eat meat not too often. More than once a month. Maybe two or three times a month. I eat sandwiches, canned tuna. Eggs is kinda like a luxury kind of thing. You buy eggs as often as you buy sirloin. Not too often." Her head was filled with mental imagery mapping out all the discount stores in the surrounding community—grubby little places in dilapidated old strip malls that sold food at even lower prices than Wal-Mart. Memories of recent on-sale finds—the tinned soups from Aldi's with lumps of grease floating in the liquid, the seventy-five-cent tuna fish cans at Big Lots—jostled with memories from back when she was married, living in the city, and her house was filled with children and there'd always be meat, fish, vegetables, salad—*real* food—in the fridge for when people came over for dinner.

"I had some oranges," she recalled with a self-deprecating smile. "They were on sale. A couple of months ago they had grapes on sale—and I bought grapes because I like grapes." When she occasionally purchased meat, it was desperately cheap and of an indeterminate cut. "All I know is it's red meat and it looks like a steak. If it's less than three dollars for a package of six steaks, that looks like a good deal to me." But deals like that didn't come along too often. Usually her diet was more prosaic. "I eat peanut butter and jelly a lot. I get ham salad in a can. I eat soup. I like chicken noodle soup. And I'll go to the less expensive stores, like Save-A-Lot, Aldi's. I'll get chicken noodle or Campbell's chunky. There's meat in there. It's like a stew. It's sixty-six cents. You can pour it over noodles and put butter on it. It's really good. It's like a delicacy. In the mornings I don't eat. I drink a cup of tea."

One hundred and fifty years ago, the British journalist Henry

Mayhew, researching his oral history book *London Labour and the London Poor*, encountered a similar use of tea as a food substitute among Victorian London's impoverished working classes. In the early twentieth century, Coca-Cola posters announced that the drink "revives and sustains" those who imbibed it. The caffeine in the soft drink performed a similarly energizing role to that in the cockney Londoner's sacred "cuppa tea."

"There's times I'm hungry, and I'll look in the refrigerator for something. I'll find a snack pudding. Some leftover rice. I usually eat at five thirty or six, on my shift. I'll just have a cup of tea," Aubretia continued. "I'm not starving or anything like that. I see people at work; there's a lot of things you can cut out. People don't have to have TV. You can live without TV. I have my Internet, so that occupies me. I have a DVD and VCR so I can watch movies. I read a lot, and lately I've been exchanging movies. When I come home at midnight, if I'm really hungry I'll have a cup of soup."

In the small southern New Mexico town of Hobbes, onetime Wal-Mart employee Jenny Hughes remembered that after sixteen years with the company she could afford health insurance for herself but not for her two boys. "One year, they gave me a nickel raise," she remembered. "How would you feel if you got a nickel raise?" Even though the family's mobile home payments only came to eighty dollars a month, by the end of each pay cycle she was broke, and the family would end up seeking money for food from her relatives.

Far north of Hobbes, in the rural community of Matton, Illinois, a longtime Wal-Mart employee reported that she'd lost so many hours in 2008 that she stood to earn three thousand dollars less than the previous year. "I had a store manager one time who sent me home with eleven hours for the week and told me to 'take a mini-vacation.' I said 'My bills are not going to take a vacation.'" And, she added bitterly, her health-care costs were piling up. "The insurance is horrendous. They pay a maximum of sixty dollars for a mammogram and pap smear. The remainder comes out of your pocket. And they will not allow it to come out of the deductible. That leaves me paying three hundred or four hundred dollars out-of-pocket." The employee was paying fifty dollars every two weeks for her health insurance and another $8.35 for supplemental cancer insurance. The extra insurance was necessary because she had a history of cancer in her family and the Wal-Mart policy wouldn't pay for her colonoscopies.

America, said Beth Shulman, author of the book *The Betrayal of Work* and codirector of the D.C.-based Fairness Initiative on Low-Wage Work, needs "proper regulations in place with regards to the Wal-Marts of the world. You could come up with a pay-or-play kind of plan. Either you provide a certain kind of basic [health-care] plan," one that would not permit the high employee contributions demanded under Wal-Mart's current plans, "or you've got to pay into a [pool] system. You've got to talk in large, broad terms about what needs to be done so that people can get back on the road to the middle class. There need to be new rules put in place. Start with the minimum wage and health care. Have people enforcing the regulations that are already there. You have to lay out an overall umbrella agenda and work away at each part of it. You've got to put it in moral terms. In value terms."

In 2004, voters in California came close to passing Proposition 72, an initiative that would have mandated something similar to Shulman's idea. Any company with more than fifty employees would have been mandated to provide health insurance to its workers. Safeway and several other companies favored such an approach. But Wal-Mart and fast-food corporations pumped huge sums of money into the No campaign. On Election Day, the measure went down by a whisker, with just under 51 percent voting against it.

Similar attempts to push expanded access to health care at a federal level also perished during these years. Many of the same companies and political figures who clamored for hundreds of billions of dollars in government money to rescue the banking system when it started to implode over the summer of 2008 had spent years arguing that universal health care was too costly, too bureaucratic, too likely to lead to the government assuming a "socialist" tinge. Yet in many ways the same arguments could be made for universal health care as were later made on behalf of the Wall Street bailout: it was a necessary societal investment that would prevent great harm coming to Main Street; it was a sensible use of taxpayer dollars that, in the long run, would save the country money.

In the post-bailout era, saying no to health-care reform suddenly made a whole lot less political sense. After all, if government money was good enough for Wall Street, why was it out of bounds when it came to giving poor people access to doctors? Government, argued Shulman, should be targeting tax credits for companies that offered expanded health insurance access; it should be issuing tax refunds to low income workers seeking insurance; and around the country state administrations should create large-scale pools, as was done in Massachusetts, to make health coverage more affordable. The goal, she believed, should ultimately be a nation in which nobody was denied health care because they didn't have deep enough pockets.

Shulman didn't want stories such as that of the New Mexico worker having to pay for her own cancer insurance. She didn't want more experiences such as those faced by so many farmworkers, their meager earnings from laboring in the fields rendering them too cash-rich for Medicaid, even though they were too poor to actually pay for care. When these men and women came down with serious illnesses, too often they couldn't fill prescriptions for life-saving medicines, or they had to resort to folk remedies for treating dangerous illnesses such as pneumonia. In some California Central Valley towns, the saying went, you could get the diagnosis; you just couldn't afford the cure. Often, people couldn't even get the diagnosis.

The lives of these uninsured and underinsured men and women were worlds away from the opportunities to live a middle-class lifestyle afforded the unionized post–World War II employees of

General Motors, Ford, General Electric, and the other industrial giants who had, until recently, dominated the top tier of the Fortune 500 list. Nowadays, a different set of rules was in play, supported and pushed for by new titans such as Wal-Mart. While the old behemoths had bought labor peace after the turbulent 1930s by agreeing to channel much of their profits into higher salaries and better benefits for their workforces, the Walton family largely horded the profits from its chain of stores. By the early years of the new century, they were sitting on a fortune estimated at $80 billion.

Such disparities—the toleration and even encouragement of growing wealth gaps between workers and executives—were light years away from Franklin Roosevelt's notion that employers had an obligation to provide wages that would afford their employees a decent shot at realizing the American Dream. In the 1930s, government officials denounced in harsh terms firms with labor practices like those later utilized by Wal-Mart. Such officials used their public platforms to push for an array of worker protections, including raising the minimum wage, making it easier to unionize, and ensuring workplace safety rules were followed.

By the 2000s, government looked at Wal-Mart, turned a blind eye to the harsh conditions, and lauded the company's success. "This is one of our nation's great companies," Vice President Dick Cheney told a group of Wal-Mart employees at their Bentonville, Arkansas, headquarters in 2004, in a speech largely devoted to pushing for more deregulation of the economy and deeper tax cuts, "and one of the most familiar names in all of America. The story of Wal-Mart exemplifies some of the very best qualities of our country—hard work, the spirit of enterprise, fair dealing, and integrity."

When the city council in Chicago overwhelmingly passed a living-wage ordinance in 2006 requiring so-called big-box stores like Wal-Mart—companies with more than $1 billion per year in revenue—to pay employees at least ten dollars per hour, plus three dollars per hour worth of benefits by the year 2010, Wal-Mart launched an extraordinary, and Orwellian, public relations campaign against the proposal. "It's sad—this puts politics ahead of working men and women. It means that Chicago is closed to business," the *New York Times* quoted a company spokesman as saying. Because it was only a citywide ordinance, with no power to impact wages elsewhere in the state, let alone nationally, Wal-Mart could, in essence, blackmail the Windy City: *Rethink your position*, the company essentially said, *or we'll take our megastores and their jobs elsewhere, to communities where people are happy to work for six or seven dollars an hour.* The message resonated. Four months later, when Chicago Mayor Richard Daley, under intense pressure from the city's business community, vetoed the measure, another Wal-Mart spokesman labeled the veto a "victory" for working families. And several aldermen who had initially supported the proposal, fearful of the consequences of a big-box withdrawal from their neighborhoods, indicated they would switch sides in a revote. The veto stood.

To be fair, though, this isn't all about Wal-Mart. The rise of the low-wage, low-benefit corporate workplace can also be attributed to the growing role of the notoriously low-paying fast-food industry, to the country's increasing reliance on casual service sector work, and to the collapse of industrial, unionized employment in America over the past thirty years.

In the 1950s, one in three American workers had manufacturing jobs, which, while physically demanding, generally paid fairly decent wages, provided health-care insurance, provided unemployment insurance in case of layoffs, and offered a guaranteed pension. Today, only one in ten employees has such a job. In 2007, the Bureau of Labor Statistics estimated that about as many, 11.2 million, now worked in "food preparation and serving related industries" with a mean average hourly wage of $9.35 and an annual salary of $19,440. The median wage data in these industries was even lower: $8.24 an hour. Fully half of food industry workers were earning less than that.

Even more Americans, 14.3 million, had sales jobs; their median hourly wage, $11.41, wasn't a whole heap better than that of food workers. And that number was somewhat inflated for most workers in this category, since it included within the computation highly paid real estate brokers, sales engineers, and managers. For cashiers, the mean hourly wage in 2007 was a paltry $8.25.

For these new employees, part-time work was common—a dodge that allowed their companies to provide health insurance to fewer people. Retirement plans generally ranged from inadequate to nonexistent, unemployment insurance usually didn't cover them, and for those who ended up working such jobs, researchers estimated these had an almost 40 percent chance of being stuck in that job for more than three years. In other words, for millions of Americans these weren't gateways to better opportunities; instead, all too often they were dead ends, walls in the way of achieving dreams. "That's a big proportion of people stuck in low-wage jobs," noted Jodie Levin-Epstein of the Center for Law and Social Policy. "We have a broken system in America for worker development. It's important to think how we can make low-wage jobs better and how we can build better pathways out of low-wage work."

By contrast, the number of billionaires in America, and the amount of wealth controlled by them, was soaring. In 2000, Forbes listed 298 American billionaires. Eight years later that number was up to 499. Globally, by 2008 there were 1,125 billionaires; even with stock market turbulence, these men and women between them controlled a staggering $4.4 trillion. Year in, year out, over the past decade the world's wealthiest individuals had accrued more money and, as significantly, gained control over a bigger percentage of global wealth. Democratic rhetoric notwithstanding, this tiny group of oligarchs controlled far more of the world's resources than did any ancien régime aristocracy. America's 499 billionaires owned over $1.5 trillion in assets. That money was equivalent to the average annual salaries of approximately 30 million of the country's workers.

Above all, America's reinvention as a low-wage economy ruled by a gilded elite can be traced to a specific political philosophy. This belief system—like the model that made the robber barons of the late nineteenth century so rich—ushered in policies that massively stacked the decks in favor of companies like Wal-Mart. At the same time, it worked against the interests of the millions of Joe-workers struggling simply to stay in place and not be swept back down the economic ladder. Aubretia Edick's diet was the unsavory by-product of the rise of a new plutocracy, of a society that concentrated wealth at the top and sprinkled crumbs among the rest.

The process involved a particularly nefarious corporate-government compromise: through reforms such as the 1996 Personal Responsibility and Work Opportunity Reconciliation Act, which replaced long-term welfare aid to the poor with the self-explanatory Temporary Aid to Needy Families program, government made welfare an increasingly stringent, humiliating fallback. As a result, a huge number of people were pushed into the minimum-wage workforce. In many states, this meant they would end up working for only the federal minimum wage, since the chambers of commerce in these states opposed higher state wage thresholds and marketed themselves to companies looking to relocate by specifically promoting low-wage laws. In return for the private sector taking these people off the hands of the state, an informal understanding emerged that a portion of the tab would still be picked up by the government, in the form of food stamps and low-income heating assistance for these new employees. (In the 1990s, however, a Republican-controlled Congress temporarily barred immigrants, both legal and illegal, from receiving food stamps.) The government also provided access to child health-care programs and even Medicaid. It was a win-win: the government reduced, though didn't entirely eliminate, its social safety net, no longer paying the full cost of welfare to the long-term unemployed and instead intervening through specific subsidies around food and health care; private companies got a whole lot of bargain-basement workers, many of whose benefits would come from the taxpayer rather than the employer; corporate profits, and share values, went up; and for a couple decades America got to post abnormally low unemployment numbers.

That so many of the low-wage workers ended up hungry at the end of the day was an unfortunate, but necessary, collateral consequence of the new social compact. And, in many instances, it was one that could be papered over by some nifty public relations actions. Sure, Wal-Mart workers in California alone were estimated to cost the public close to $90 million a year in public assistance, but Wal-Mart could get a whole bunch of easy-to-understand props from donating a few thousand dollars here, a few more there, to local scout groups and teacher-of-the-year programs, or—begrudgingly—from trucking in food to pantries. In December 2007 Wal-Mart announced it would provide more than 3 million meals to food banks around America, sending out one truck crammed with food to each of the fifty states.

By 2008, Wal-Mart's foundation was distributing over $300 million a year to charities around the world; it was a huge amount of money—or at least it seemed so until it was compared to the company's annual profits. That $300 million wasn't much more than 2 percent of the chain's outlandishly high profits in 2007. And it contrasted miserably with the $65 billion that Bill and Melinda Gates and Warren Buffett had injected into the Gates Foundation over the previous few years. Like Wal-Mart, many other major low-wage corporations had a similar emphasis on relatively small, but cosmetically pleasing, good deeds. McDonald's ran the much-lauded Ronald McDonald Houses for sick children, and was at the forefront of hurricane relief drives after Katrina wrecked New Orleans in 2005. In 2007, Accor North America, a company that owned downscale hotel chains such as Motel 6 and Red Roof Inn, made a $375,000 donation to educational groups working on environmental issues. In and of themselves, these donations were all worthy, and many people's lives were clearly improved by them. The problem wasn't necessarily the motives of grant makers at Wal-Mart's foundation; it was more a structural problem. That so many people needed to fall back on food pantries, partially stocked by surplus Wal-Mart food or staffed by McDonald's volunteers, was at least partly because Wal-Mart and McDonald's were pushing a peculiarly exploitative business model into front-center stage of the economy.

An hour outside Boise, Idaho, in the Wild West–styled former gold-mining camp of Idaho City, Allen and his wife, Karyl, were living in a large house on the edge of the woods. The house belonged to Karyl's mom. Since moving from Fort Worth, Texas, three years earlier in 2002, Allen and Karyl had been struggling to make ends meet. Active members of the Church of Jesus Christ of Latter-day Saints, the couple had six young children, and the large family was trying to survive on Allen's salary as a correctional officer. It was hard, since he was paid only slightly over eleven dollars an hour. Even with a couple hundred dollars a month extra thrown in because of his work as a communications specialist in the Army Reserves, the income barely covered the family's bills, let alone their food. They strained under the weight of medical and dental insurance premiums, car insurance, student loans, and mortgage payments on an undeveloped plot of land they had bought using a small insurance settlement for the down payment.

Most of the family's food, the couple estimated, came from donations made by their church. Allen felt ashamed of this, but his shame was dulled somewhat by the fact that he was also a volunteer at the pantry, helping others as well as receiving food. It was also mitigated because he knew that several of his coworkers at the prison were in similar straits. Some lived with parents or in-laws because their salaries didn't provide enough to pay rent. Several others were using local food pantries. "But we don't talk about it," he added, embarrassment written on his face. "They don't know I rely on it."

On paper, Idaho was thriving in 2005. It had an unemployment rate of 4 percent, considerably lower than the national average. It boasted one of the highest rates of population growth of any state in the country, and it touted its high level of economic growth. Yet the jobs that were being created at breakneck speed were not paying the bills. Private sector work generally paid poorly; state tax revenues were, in consequence, low, and as a result state employees such as Allen also ended up getting the short end of the stick. "It has to do with the cost of fuel, the cost of housing," said Rescue Mission executive director Bill Roscoe. "People are working but not earning enough money to meet their needs. For me to pay another fifty cents a gallon for gas isn't a big deal. For someone earning eight dollars an hour with two children, it's a huge deal. We help a lot of people find work, and I'd say, on average, the starting wage is nine to eleven dollars per hour. And those are pretty good jobs. Probably a majority of people living in this valley make less than that."

As the price of gas went up, Allen found he could no longer afford to make the daily commute from his mother-in-law's home in Idaho City to his job as a correctional officer near Boise. And so the thirty-four-year-old began staying on a military reserve base three or four nights a week, leaving his wife and kids behind, returning only on weekends and for his Cub Scouts volunteer work on Wednesday evenings. Even so, by 2005, with gas up near $2.50 a gallon, 20 percent of his after-tax income was going on fuel. In the years following, that number would likely have spiraled up to well over one-third.

While Allen struggled to provide for his family on an hourly wage of eleven dollars and change, many of Idaho's residents were even worse off. Roscoe recalled one woman the Rescue Mission gave a turkey to for Christmas who worked seventy hours a week—as a secretary for a local attorney and as a salesperson at the local Wal-Mart—and still couldn't afford to feed herself and her two children. Another woman emailed the food bank to say that she and her husband "get to spend about $120 every two months on groceries and eat a lot of toast to chase the hunger away. We don't get fresh fruits and vegetables, or cereals and milk. Those are luxury items. I am just a little fed up with sending my husband to work with no lunch, with no dinner."

Into the 1990s, Idaho—which back in the late nineteenth and early twentieth centuries had been a hotbed of radical, sometimes violent, labor organizing and politics—was a politically competitive state. Some years Democrats were in charge, winning power with the support of union voters in the timber and mining industries in particular; other years, the Republicans would win. But in the 1980s the state began heading in a more conservative direction, with voters passing an antiunion Right to Work ballot initiative in 1986; and by the early 1990s, as union power waned, the party of the donkeys was rapidly losing influence. The last Democratic governor left office in Boise in 1994, and since then conservative Republicans, riding the national wave of "morals" politics, and using the antigovernment rhetoric of Reagan and Bush, had controlled the entire state apparatus. While they talked the talk on abortion, creationism, guns, gays, and the other issues that generally fired up conservative evangelical voters, much of their political energy was actually spent remaking Idaho's economy.

By early in the new century, Idaho had some of the lowest state taxes in the country and was attracting a fair share of new, high-tech corporations to replace jobs lost in the declining resource-extraction industries. Micron and Hewlett-Packard were among the companies to establish campuses in the state. Yet, because of the low tax base, even with the presence of these titans of the new economy, the state found itself increasingly unable to fund basic public services. It was notoriously reluctant to support state welfare programs, and kicked a higher percentage of its welfare recipients off welfare in the year following Bill Clinton's signing of the 1996 welfare reform act than did any other state. Making matters worse, in 2000 the legislature mandated that public agencies *not* inform clients about how to access state services.

Idaho represented a particularly Social Darwinist vision of America's future, a future in which a few thrived while many sank into poverty: hollow out state welfare services, reduce worker protections, let the minimum wage lose purchasing power, and export goods-producing jobs overseas while leaving the lower strata of the U.S. workforce ever more dependent on dead-end service sector employment. "There's a schizophrenia about taxes and services," explained Sam Blair of the Idaho Community Action Network, sitting over a cold beer in one of Boise's several Basque eateries. "It's a framing of the issue that divorces taxes from the services which taxes sustain." And thus the strange, though increasingly common, spectacle of rising hunger among working families in the middle of an economic boom. "If you look at the average family income in Idaho," explained Dick Schultz, administrator of the State Division of Health, "you'll see the income is quite low compared to other states. The job market here is not necessarily the high-end job market."

During the first half of the 1980s, the Virginia-based National Right to Work Committee began targeting states that it thought were politically ripe for an assault on trade union power. In one state after another, mainly in the South, and then, increasingly, in the West—in states that were swinging into the conservative political bloc that formed the bedrock of Reaganism—the committee either pushed sympathetic legislators to propose Right to Work laws or itself organized initiative campaigns. By 1985, twenty states had passed laws gutting union power in the workplace and affirming that, even in places where a union contract was in effect and its protections covered all employees, workers couldn't be mandated to pay union dues.

Idaho was the twenty-first state the committee went after, its operations coordinated by a roving political consultant named Bill Wilson. At the time, Idaho had a Democratic governor, and, when the Republican-controlled legislature passed Right to Work, he promptly vetoed it. Undeterred, the committee immediately launched an initiative campaign. Their language was, from the get-go, disingenuous. Idaho's economy had been in deep trouble since the Carter years, and many Idahoans came to believe, with prompting from pro–Right to Work advertisements, that the proposed law would literally guarantee them employment. On Election Day, the measure narrowly passed, and soon afterward stories started surfacing of people going into company offices and demanding work, believing the new law locked in place a right to the job of their choice—only to be told the companies weren't hiring.

As it turned out, 1986 was the high-water mark for the Right to Work movement. Idaho was the last state to pass Right to Work for fifteen years, until 2001. Then, amid a new assault on unions and union-negotiated contracts, and conservative Republicans in Congress and organizations such as the Heritage Foundation pushing for passage of a National Right to Work Act, the committee managed to convince Oklahoma to enact such legislation.

Despite coming in late, though, Idaho's law profoundly altered the state's labor conditions. The new law banned the union closed shop and set in motion a barrage of other changes that cumulatively eroded trade union power in the once-strong organized labor state, lowered wages, and made it harder for unions to maintain strong benefits packages when negotiating contracts. In 1985, about 22 percent of Idaho's workforce was unionized. Twenty years later, the state chapter of the AFL-CIO estimated, that number was closer to 9 percent.

Shortly after the initiative, the Democrats went into a tailspin, not least because unions had been so constricted in what sorts of political activities they could engage in. Bill Wilson reportedly told a rival political consultant that his campaign had, as a by-product, "killed off" the state's Democratic machine.

The newly ascendant Republicans repealed the state's prevailing

wage statute. This statute, known as Little Davis-Bacon—a reference to the federal Davis-Bacon prevailing wage laws—mandated
contractors working for the state pay their employees wages no lower
than those paid to similarly skilled workers in the private sector.
They also banned public employees' unions from making political
contributions and engaging in voter outreach campaigns aimed
at reaching nonunion members, blocked increases in the state's
minimum wage, and ended the paying of mandatory overtime if an
employee worked more than eight hours in a given day. At the same
time, the state's Supreme Court consistently upheld the state's "fire-
at-will" provisions that allowed employers to terminate nonunion
employees without good cause. The court's justices, it's worth not-
ing, were directly elected by an increasingly conservative populace—
or at least one in which the minority who bothered to vote voted
conservatively, in an era in which the participatory political culture
fostered by trade unionism was being destroyed.

"We're the testing grounds," explained union organizer Dave
Whaley, in his offices on the outskirts of Boise. A big man in a
brightly checkered wool shirt and jeans, with a white walrus mustache and neatly parted gray hair, Whaley believed Right to Work
had profoundly changed the state's political culture. "We're the
places antiworker rules are brought. And if they work they take them
to other states and try to ram them down their throats as well."

Less tangibly, since unions still had to represent nonunion members in any workplace in which a union-negotiated contract held
sway, the incentives for joining a trade union and participating in
its organizing work declined. "Why?" one fifty-year-old union organizer in Lewiston recalls a colleague responding when asked whether
he wanted to join the union, an act that would have cost him forty-
six dollars per month in union dues. "I can get the exact same as you
for nothing." As a result, the culture of union participation began to
break down. Within a few years, there were supermarkets in Idaho
that were technically union workplaces, but which had virtually no

union members among the staff. The same held in some of the old timber mills and paper-pulping facilities. "The longer it goes, the less in touch your children are with what they have lost," said Cindy Hedge, the treasurer of the Citizens Committee to Repeal Right to Work, whose son worked a nonunion job as a manager at a Petco store for just over ten dollars an hour. "The leadership isn't educating our children."

Some in Idaho recognized that their ostensibly populist state leaders had done a snow job on them. In 2003, trade unions launched a campaign to repeal the 1986 Right to Work law. The petition drive gathered enough signatures—6 percent of the state's registered voters—to place an initiative on the ballot, but during the certification process county clerks disallowed thousands of them, and so the measure wasn't voted on in 2004. While the campaign was underway, though, drivers on Interstate 90 heading west across the state line from Coeur d'Alene to Spokane, Washington, would come across a billboard reading "If Right to Work is so good, why are you working in Washington?" The sign was alluding to the fact that so many Idahoans were trying to find jobs in the nearby state of Washington, which had enacted a minimum wage more than two dollars per hour higher than the federal one, and which had far higher pay rates for skilled workers in fields such as construction.

Two years later, and despite the fact the I-90 billboard was now hosting an advertisement for a local Hooters restaurant, the unions tried and failed again. Their signature-gathering effort was a grassroots, bare-bones affair, their opponents massively outspending them to get their antiunion message across to voters. Residents of gritty northern towns like Coeur d'Alene and Lewiston supported the measure; residents of the southern cities of Boise and Idaho Falls, where the new high-tech and service jobs were concentrated, didn't. Despite Idaho State University pollsters' estimate that upward of half the electorate supported repeal, the organizers couldn't muster sufficient resources to get enough petition gatherers out statewide. Even if they had, they would likely have been blitzkrieged by well-funded antiunion industry groups come election time.

"The basic reason for Right to Work is to enhance economic development by making it possible for companies to compete with [those in] other states and internationally," argued Steve Ahrens, of the solidly antiunion Idaho Association of Commerce and Industry, sitting in his office in downtown Boise. His collection of model classic cars was proudly displayed on his shelves. "It's an important part of our economic development basket of incentives. And the business community will seek to retain it."

Of course, the economic development that Ahrens touted was, at best, of a dubious nature. Idaho's unskilled workers were having to work for the sorts of rock-bottom wages one generally associates with a maquiladora zone, such as in border towns like Juárez, Mexico. Unemployment *was* low, but that didn't mean workers were being paid anything approaching livable wages. While the federal minimum wage was $5.15 per hour in 2006 when the Repeal Right to Work campaign was underway, restaurants in Idaho, unlike in neighboring states, were still allowed to pay workers barely three dollars, with the shortfall between that and the minimum wage supposedly being made up for by tips.

Not surprisingly, the low-end fast-food chains and food stands along roads like 21st Street in Lewiston paid workers wages that did not even begin to cover the normal costs of living. Idaho had one of the lowest median wages in the country and came in dead last in wages for female workers. Wal-Marts, call centers, communications companies, and other boom employers paid entry-level wages that barely reached seven dollars per hour. And, even during the now long-gone boom times, food pantries were reporting increasing levels of hunger, not just among the unemployed—who received some of the worst welfare benefits in the country—but also, increasingly, among the working poor.

Similar stories held throughout much of the country. Idaho represented the northwestern point of a low-wage arc. From there, you could head south to Utah, through New Mexico (which, despite the living-wage ordinance in Santa Fe and the minimum-wage movement in Albuquerque, was home to some of the poorest counties in the country), into Texas, east through the states of the Old South, then up through Appalachia toward the Eastern Seaboard. All along that arc were states that had resisted establishing higher minimum wages during the long years the federal minimum wage had stagnated, states that had adopted Right to Work laws that made unionization harder for workers, and states whose chambers of commerce had lured businesses with breathy promises of lower labor bills.

"We're leaving behind people who are considered at the lower end of middle class," Natalie Jayroe, president and CEO of the Second Harvest Food Bank of Greater New Orleans and Acadiana, argued. "These are the people getting squeezed." In some rural parishes in Louisiana, where almost half the post–Hurricane Katrina population lived in poverty, lines for the mobile food pantries that drove into hard-to-reach areas of the bayou formed hours before the trucks were due to arrive. "I'm distributing twenty million pounds of food a year," Jayroe said. "I'd like to be distributing fifty million pounds." Faced with higher gas prices, hefty surcharges tacked on to utility bills in the wake of Katrina, and devastating rebuilding costs, entire communities were coming to rely on aid. Jayroe had even heard reports from her staff of firefighters standing in line for food.

But it wasn't just recent hurricane damage that caused the hunger. Poverty and malnutrition had long been Achilles' heels for Louisiana, as also for neighboring Mississippi and Alabama. African American slaves and their descendants had, over centuries, endured conditions unthinkable to most Americans outside the South. So, too, had white tenant farmers, the skin-and-bones families who lived in the humble shacks photographed by Walker Evans and written about by James Agee in their classic book *Let Us Now Praise*

Famous Men. During the Civil War and its aftermath, families in the South literally starved. A century later, in the 1960s, babies with the bloated bellies associated with extreme malnutrition could still be seen in remoter communities throughout the region.

Labor in the Deep South has long been considered expendable, and those with money have long resisted paying for the adequate funding of social programs. For decades, those who decried this social order were labeled "uppity" and deemed to be "agitators." The waves of lynching that swept the states of the ex-Confederacy in the late nineteenth and early twentieth centuries were, concluded the African American journalist Ida B. Wells, as much about stomping on the economic aspirations of freed black men and women as they were about using terror to eradicate perceived transgressions of the Jim Crow sexual code.

The Southern business model condemned low-end workers throughout the entire South, a huge swathe of land not far shy of 1 million square miles, to poverty. At least, in Idaho, those with connections and the money to commute across state lines daily had some chance of still earning decent wages. In the decades following passage of Right to Work, a growing number of skilled workers in the construction trades began driving to nearby towns, just across the state lines, in the non–Right to Work states of Oregon and Washington, where wage rates were, in many industries, about five dollars per hour higher, or close to ten thousand dollars a year more than in Idaho—even for Idaho's remaining unionized tradesmen. In 1988 alone, the state's Department of Labor estimated that five thousand construction workers left Idaho. In 2000, researchers from the University of Idaho found that skilled workers were leaving the state faster than younger workers were being trained to replace them. "We lost the cream of the crop," explained Jim Kerns, ex-head of the state's AFL-CIO. "They went to other states to make a living." Yet, said Shirl Boyce, vice president of economic development for the Boise Chamber of Commerce, companies looking to relocate to Idaho routinely told him, "If you're not Right to Work, we're not interested in coming to your area." And so, wages continued to stagnate. "We've seen long periods of time where we haven't gained in terms of benefits and wages. We haven't been able to bargain even for the cost of living [increase]," Jim Wallace, of the Pacific Northwest Regional Council of Carpenters, explained. "It's pretty sad when you've got a state advertising its cheap labor. That's not what it's about."

In the 1990s, Idaho was somewhere in the mid range nationwide as far as hunger went. Less than a decade later, according to studies by the U.S. Department of Agriculture and Brandeis University's Center on Hunger and Poverty, Idaho, along with its southern neighbor, Utah, were among the very worst in the country. From 2001 through 2003, before the poverty numbers began rising nationally again, 11 percent of Americans were reporting food insecurity (a slight decline from 11.3 percent in the late 1990s), but the figure for Idahoans was 13.7 percent. And while 3.4 percent of the country was reporting actual hunger, Idahoans came in at 3.9 percent. In a seven-year period, from the late 1990s to the mid-2000s, years when Idaho was supposedly booming, the official hunger rate in the state had increased by over 20 percent, with all the indications being that things were only going to get worse.

Food banks and other charities noticed the difference. In 2000, the Boise Rescue Mission gave out about six hundred Christmas turkeys. Four years later, more than eighteen hundred families received them. In 2003, the Idaho Food Bank distributed slightly more than 4 million pounds of food. In 2004, that number was 5.5 million pounds. "Idaho is the sixth worst hunger state in the nation," explained Kathy Gardner, agency relations specialist with the food bank. Then, as the national economy started to wobble, Idaho's hunger data got even worse. Food pantries began reporting shortages in meats, eggs, and other protein-filled foods as donors struggled to keep up with the exploding need. In Pocatello, volunteers were temporarily reduced to giving out only crackers and frozen potatoes. Mobile pantries reported being mobbed by hungry residents. An eighty-seven-year-old man in Blackfoot was reported to have stood in line for two hours waiting for his mobile pantry box. By 2008, the Idaho Food Bank was detailing increases of 20 percent a year in the demand for charity food. In the affluent community of Sun Valley, the food bank saw a threefold increase in the number of clients from 2007 to 2008. That same year the number of Idaho residents on food stamps jumped by more than 14 percent.

Then, an even more disturbing trend emerged. Schools documented a rising number of impoverished children needing free school breakfasts and lunches. In schools like Van Buren Elementary School, in a downscale neighborhood of Caldwell, 90 percent of the children qualified for free meals by mid-2008. Some estimates put the number at 98 percent, said school Principal Lavaun Dennett. Summer feeding programs for children, put in place in the late 1960s to provide kids from poor families with food during the months when school was out, also began reporting startling increases in the numbers of hungry children.

In the belt of poor towns west of Boise, the Reverend Royce Wright ran a summer feeding program through his Oasis Food and Worship Center. In the summer of 2006, his team gave out 178,000 free meals to children in nine cities in the area. The following summer, they handed out just over 200,000 lunches and dinners. In 2008, that number had climbed again, to about a quarter of a million. "I was talking to a mother at the beginning of the season," recalled the pastor, a fiery, almost messianic man in his late fifties. Royce had had a full life. In his youth, working as a diesel mechanic, he veered into alcoholism. Then, in the 1970s, he found God, enrolled in Bible school, and become a preacher. More recently, Royce had begun flying to Africa once a year, going off alone into the countryside of Tanzania, Kenya, Uganda, Rwanda, and South

Africa to preach the gospel. In Idaho, Royce—with his burly phy-
sique and at-ease approach to his staff—acquired a reputation as a
go-to guy for helping people in need. "She [the mother]said, 'Royce,
we're a family of six. And we've cut back in every way we can cut
back, and we're still not making it.' There's a big segment of people
who are working poor out there. It's a decision between putting gas
in the car and buying food. When we think of hunger, we think of
Africa—little kids with distended stomachs. In America, it's a different mentality. We're talking about food insecurity. Because of the
networks we have, we're able to not have full-blown hunger. But we
have food insecurity. There's children who go to bed every night not
knowing where their next meal is coming from. Or they go to bed
with chips and soda pops. A gallon of milk is over three dollars."

By the summer of 2008, however, the insecurity was metamor-
phosing into real food shortages, as overstretched charities struggled
to keep up with exploding demand.

When researchers from Boise State University's Center for
Environmental Sensing asked young children on the breadlines to
draw crayon pictures about hunger, the results were staggering: one
little boy drew a sad stick figure, "holding his stomach because it
hurts." Another child drew a sad little girl. *Her reason for being sad?*
the researchers asked. There was no food to eat in the dumpster. A
third picture was of a boy's stomach, colored dark because, the child
explained, the boy was hungry. There was a picture of a boy stranded
on an island, with the emergency message "hungry" written into
the sands on the beach. Finally, there was a picture of a mom and
her son; the mom was crying because the family had no food in the
house. They weren't stick figures, the young artist explained, just
skinny people who hadn't eaten.

About a mile from Van Buren Elementary school, Luby Park nestled
against an embankment under the highway. It was a large park,
mainly open grass, a kid's playground off to one side, a small rose

garden at its northern edge. All summer long, workers for the local feeding program would drive up to the parking lot on the edge of the rose patch just before lunch and again before dinner. They would set up a table, unload their bags and boxes of food—greasy corndogs, slices of pizza, quesadillas, little milk cartons, fruits, carrots, peanuts—and prepare to serve the local kids.

Some of the children would hang out in the park all afternoon, their free meals the focal point of their day. Others would be brought by their parents, or they would cycle or walk to the rose garden with their friends; they'd come at the beginning of the meal hour, stand patiently in line for their food, and make a picnic of it on the lawn or at one of the tables that dotted the park. There was a sort of Norman Rockwell quality to the scene—except for the fact that the ragamuffin young 'uns were being sustained by charity. None of the children refused food; none said they didn't like pizza or corn dogs. They took what they were given and went off to eat. Maybe they weren't really hungry but just felt like spending an hour playing with friends in the park, with the added bonus of free food thrown in. Or maybe they knew enough of a good thing to not make brats of themselves while waiting in line. For whatever reasons, the lines were orderly and the children well mannered.

But then there was the jalopy rush: the line of beaten-up, paint-dulled old cars, mud-spattered minivans, and hand-me-down SUVs that began snaking toward the rose garden parking lot in the last few minutes of the hour. The parents would park their cars; the children would jump out, run up to the table, take their free food, and rush back to the vehicles. And the adults would drive them home. For them, there was no "maybe." These boys and girls were hungry, plain and simple; they weren't coming to the park to play. For them it was just a pit stop. And if the feeding program table wasn't there, they wouldn't eat.

Throughout the long summer months, more that one hundred children would come to Luby Park for food each day in the middle of the week—even when it rained, dozens of kids would still be standing in line. On Fridays, when the parents got paid, the numbers would drop off. By the time the program closed for the season, in mid-August, Luby Park alone had seen thousands of meals handed out. And the park was just one of dozens of free feeding locales in the territory laid claim to by Reverend Wright.

And yet, despite spreading inequality and poverty, a myth persists, or at least *did* persist until the 2008 financial meltdown and trillion-dollar bailout of Wall Street forced Americans to look more carefully at who gained and who lost in early twenty-first-century America. The myth was twofold: first, that America remained a classless society, or at least an overwhelmingly middle-class society. And second, that everyone should consume as if money were no object. Because most people viewed themselves as upwardly mobile, they would consume according to limits set by their aspirations rather than their bank balances, even if they had to go into ever-greater debt to keep up with the Joneses.

America's is a culture of mass consumption. Over several decades, notions of citizenship have been re-crafted to reflect the centrality of shopping and consuming in our lives. In many ways, the fruits of early-twenty-first-century American citizenship were seen in terms of the purchasing power afforded the country's population. Witness George Bush's bizarre instructions to Americans shortly after the September 11th, 2001, terrorist attacks: *Don't let the terrorists win*, the president told his audience. *Do your patriotic duty. Go out and shop.*

The result of this new understanding of a citizen's rights and obligations was that a tremendous premium—and psychological pressure via advertising—was placed on a person's ability to spend money, even if in spending that money families destroyed their own fragile financial balancing act. How else to explain poor people buying sports utility vehicles even as gas rose toward four dollars a gallon, families going into steep credit card debt to purchase enormous flat screen TVs, young kids in working-class neighborhoods going to school wearing two-hundred-dollar sneakers?

We consume in response to signals sent out by large-scale political and economic institutions. And for many years we, as a society, were given the wrong signals. It is too easy to blame individuals for making bad choices. Sure, people bought more fripperies than they should have, but they did so with more than a nod and a wink from government officials, financiers, and businessmen who should have known better.

Instead of placing limits on how far into credit card debt families could plunge themselves, or what kind of interest rates and fees they could be charged, government stepped back, let more and more families go further into the hole, and essentially deregulated the credit industry. Instead of stepping in to make the minimum wage more akin to a living wage—or enforcing, at a national level, big-box statutes that would push large-scale employers such as Wal-Mart to pay wages that would allow workers to live decently without borrowing or falling back on state assistance and charity—the government allowed the value of the minimum wage to erode. The assumption was that workers could continually make up the shortfall by either working longer hours or normalizing credit card borrowing as a central part of their financial calculus. Instead of making more low-income workers eligible for heating assistance, the Earned Income Tax Credit (EITC), and other subsidies, key measures of poverty were kept artificially low. Increasingly, the new working poor found themselves deemed too affluent to partake in such programs. All too often, as a result, borrowed money came to fill the gaps in poor Americans' budgets, and a culture of debt came to be seen almost as a social good.

Caught in this somewhat delusional narrative, the political culture veered rightward. Sure, tax cuts proposed by Republicans might flow overwhelmingly toward the already rich and might denude basic social services, but there was always the chance that, while poor today, you, too, might someday soon leap into that favored club. All you needed was one good chance, one ball thrown into your strike zone for you to belt right out of the park. "We compare ourselves not to our neighbors but to characters we see on TV who are able to afford status brand lifestyles," explained Michelle Nelson, associate professor of advertising at the Urbana-Champaign campus of the University of Illinois. "We're always striving to get to that next level, which is pretty much beyond our means. It is products that give us our identity, our lifestyles, help us choose our friends." Over a period of decades, Nelson argued, "conspicuous consumption [became] more of a norm. What becomes the norm for your social class shifts. The notion of consumption [becomes] related to patriotism."

And in such a cultural environment, why *not* support people advocating lower taxes for the rich? After all you, too, could one day be wealthy; and when you were you'd need as much disposable income as possible to fuel your consumption-driven journey up the social ladder. "By the end of the 1990s," wrote Harvard professor Juliet Schor, in her much-acclaimed book *The Overspent American*, "the familiar elements of the American Dream (a little suburban house with a white picket fence, two cars, and an annual vacation) [had] expanded greatly. The size of houses has doubled in less than fifty years, there are more second homes, automobiles have become increasingly option-packed, middle-income Americans are doing more pleasure and vacation travel, and expenditures on recreation have more than doubled since 1980."

But, Schor continued, no matter how much modern-day Americans consumed, as they looked at role models on TV, at wealthier neighbors and more affluent colleagues, they felt like they weren't accessing all of the newly-minted necessities of life, and thus they dug themselves ever further into debt in order to sustain purchasing habits that their incomes alone couldn't provide for. "Thus, the new consumerism has led to a kind of mass 'overspending' within the middle class. By this I mean that large numbers of Americans spend more than they say they would like to, and more than they have. That they spend more than they realize they are spending, and more than is fiscally prudent."

And so, the "good life" became increasingly defined in terms of material possessions. That huge swathe of the population self-defined as the "American middle class"—an amorphous group that ranged from factory workers and mailmen through to accountants and lawyers—who were aspiring to the lifestyles of the rich and famous, began to identify more and more with the political and economic goals of the wealthiest few.

This identification was, in many ways, a peculiarly large-scale version of the Stockholm Syndrome, in which victims start to identify with the agenda of the people putting them in harm's way. And it came with tangible, and extremely negative, consequences. At a macro level, it put the entire financial system at risk. A decade-plus of banks falling over themselves to lend money to unqualified borrowers desperate to secure their middle-class footing ultimately resulted in the near-meltdown of the entire global financial edifice and a cascading crisis of confidence in the pillars of the American economy. At an individual level, too often it led to political choices—large numbers of economically vulnerable people voting for politicians advocating deregulation and tax cuts for the wealthy—that resulted in families eventually running out of money for food, medicine, electricity, and telephone service. It ended up magnifying the extent of poverty and the distress this caused, making hunger that much more of an epidemic than would otherwise be the case.

Think yourself rich—or at least potentially rich—and you're likely to tolerate the shredding of the social safety net. After all, with home values rising and wallets bulging with credit cards, who needed to worry about the technical stuff—the falling value of the minimum wage, the cumbersome nature of unemployment insurance, the under-enforcement of workplace safety regulations? If the market could be counted on to fix all ills, then if you were still poor it was probably somehow your own fault; and if you needed to visit the food pantry, well, you'd do it on the hush-hush and QT, full of shame lest your neighbors find out your personal failings.

Of course, we know now this only makes sense if you're operating on an assumption of permanent growth, of an economy providing decent jobs and adequate money to the vast majority of residents, of an American Dream in which upward mobility is a dominant motif instead of a dying memory. And we now know that this isn't the case. In fact, during the last decades of the twentieth and first decade of the twenty-first century, much of the rest of the industrial world became more socially mobile than America. "Social mobility is now less fluid in the United States than in other affluent nations," wrote the authors of a 2008 report commissioned by the charity Oxfam. "A poor child born in Germany, France, Canada, or one of the Nordic countries has a better chance to join the middle class in adulthood than an American child born into similar circum-stances." In 2007 UNICEF ranked America next to last in a group of twenty-one industrial nations when it came to child well-being. It stood at thirty-fourth in its infant mortality numbers, with poor children far more likely to die than affluent children. And it came in forty-second in life expectancy data, again largely because so many poor people, lacking access to medical care, die young in America.

Underpinning all this bad news? An extraordinary difference of wealth between the haves and have-nots. The top 1 percent of Americans controlled one-third of the country's wealth; the bottom 60 percent of households, just 4 percent of the money.

■ ■ ■

Interlude IV

The peculiar dull ache of hungriness, referred
to the epigastrium, is usually the organism's first
strong demand for food; and when the initial
order is not obeyed, the sensation is likely to grow
into a highly uncomfortable pang or gnawing, less
definitely localized as it becomes more intense.
This may be regarded as the essential feature of
hunger. Besides the dull ache, however, lassitude
and drowsiness may appear, or faintness, or violent
headache, or irritability and restlessness such that
continuous effort in ordinary affairs becomes
increasingly difficult.

—Walter B. Cannon, *Bodily Changes in Pain, Hunger, Fear and Rage*

I put off visiting the food pantry as a client until I had almost
finished writing my book, until I literally had run out of days to
procrastinate.

Finally, in mid-November, as I was finishing the manuscript for
this book, I let my supplies of eatables dwindle, woke up one morning, made myself a cup of coffee, ate nothing, and headed off to the
pantry. It was a sunny day, and, despite the acid feeling in my belly,
I decided to walk. Many of the food pantry clients in urban areas
either don't own cars or can't afford to drive them anymore.

There's something almost indescribable about throwing oneself
on charity, even if you know, intellectually, that it's only an experi-

ment, even if you know you're not really "one of those people." It still feels shameful. And as I walked the two miles to the food pantry, waves of panic washed over me several times. I wanted to turn around; a couple times I almost *did* turn around. I wanted to hide, to be as anonymous and secretive as possible. I felt like a man being propelled toward an appointment with a dentist for a root canal.

I reached the food bank building at 9:45 a.m. The pantry's opening time each weekday morning was 10:00, but already twenty-three people were lined up ahead of me, snaking along the outside of the spiked iron fence surrounding the food bank loading area. They were young and old, black, white, and brown; some of the women had young children with them. A few had cycled in on old bikes; others were in line with backpacks or rusted old suitcase trolleys on which they'd carry back home their precious bags of food. They stood, in the main silently, shoulders hunched, staring at the backs of the people in front of them. Each minute brought more hungry supplicants. By the time the gate was unlocked at 10:03, at least fifty people were standing in that line.

We went through the gate, then down a narrow exterior passageway. To our right were the bricks of the food bank's outer wall; to our left were the tall curved stakes of the iron fence; above us was a corrugated metal roof overhang. It was dark and claustrophobic and felt like what I imagine the queue into a workhouse must have been like in Victorian England. So many people were ahead of me that I didn't get inside straight away; the line of ragged men and women stopped while I was still in the outer passage. And even though it was warm, I shivered.

Then it started again. I inched forward, turned right through the heavy metal door. I stopped at the table with whittled-down pencils and short charity request forms to fill in. Once inside, I made a U-turn, going back down the interior side of the brick wall that I had just advanced along from the outside. To my left was a painted wall with a sheet of metal, etched with years of graffiti; to my right, dull white-and-blue painted bricks. It was even darker now, a grim institutional dimness, and the sneezes and coughs and snuffles of the people in the line reverberated as if in an echo chamber. This wasn't a supermarket without cash registers, a consumer palace of choice, of lifestyles realized. It was, I felt, rather a place for the spreading of tuberculosis or the flu, as well as every other germ, real and imagined; it was truly a last-stop hotel, a room where dignity came to die. I listened to the coughing and tried to bury my head in my coat. Inside, away from the stares of the non-poor people driving and walking along the streets near the food bank, the silence of the line was replaced with loud, often aggressive conversations, barked-out words, harsh bravado laughter bouncing off the concrete floor.

I reached the first bulletproof window at 10:45, my back aching from standing for an hour, my nerves frayed. I had worked on the other side of that window months earlier as a volunteer. I remembered that, from the inside, it was an airy, well-lit place, the bustle of the helpers filling the warehouse with a sense of can-do good cheer. From the other side of that window, though, it was a grim endurance test. I gave the young man my form and my driver's license as proof of identity. I was supposed to have also brought a recent utility bill, to prove I still lived where my license said I lived. But I'd forgotten it and the volunteer kindly entered me into the computer anyway. "Bring it next time," he said gently.

I moved along to the benches attached to the wall and sat down to wait for another volunteer to process my order and call me up to collect my food at the next window. Nobody asked me what I wanted, if I was a vegetarian, whether I had allergies, if I was kosher, or diabetic, if I was lactose intolerant, or unable to ingest MSG. Nobody asked me if I was having a nice day, or engaged in any of the other small talk that makes shopping in a supermarket so deliberately, if artificially, pleasant. I was, quite simply, a *case*.

"Sasha?" a middle-aged woman called out a few minutes later. When I came up to the open window, she handed me six green plastic bags, knotted at the top. "These are for you," she said, her voice half a gift and half a warning cry of condescension. I gathered them up gratefully, stuffed them into the canvas tote bags I'd brought with me, painfully aware of the fact that probably half of the food would be inedible, and shambled off back home.

It was, without a doubt, the most joyless shopping experience of my life; but I was hungry and wanted to return to my kitchen to rip open the bags and see what food items the guardian angels had sent my way.

FIVE

Elderly, Angry, and Looking for Work

You can't eat the orange and throw the peel
away—a man is not a piece of fruit.
—Arthur Miller, *Death of a Salesman*, Act II (1949)

FOR TOM HAZEL, UNIVERSAL HEALTH CARE and income protections for low-wage workers couldn't come too soon. But, at the same time, whenever they did come, in many ways they'd already be too late. The 2000s hadn't been kind to Hazel and his friends, and no matter what changes might sweep the post-Bush nation, realistically their best days were likely behind them. It wasn't just that they were facing the middle-aged blues; it was that the promises made to them had been broken and the ballast stabilizing their lives thrown overboard.

Hazel was a tall man in his early fifties, with a red face, glasses, and a graying but once-ginger goatee beard. On the Saturday before Labor Day, 2006, sitting in the Longview, Washington, office of the United Steelworkers, he was casually dressed in a Cardinals' baseball cap, black T-shirt, and shorts.

Longview was a 1920s-era industrial town, replete with grandiose stone period-piece buildings. Originally built as a "planned city" to house lumber workers and their families, its streets lead into and around green parks and open spaces. Over the decades it has succumbed to the grit that characterized most other factory communities. By early in the new century it felt tired, old, similar in feel to the polluted northern Idaho towns that had recently waged a failed war to repeal Right to Work in their state. The stone buildings whispered of past grandeur, but the whispers were growing fainter by the day.

The town lay a third of the way up the I-5 corridor from Portland to Seattle and a stone's throw west of the Mount St. Helens volcano. And until recently it had been one of the country's great aluminum-producing hubs. If you were lucky enough to get a job in the huge foundry on the edge of town, you had your ticket into the middle class. You'd likely be able to afford one of the small suburban homes with a square patch front yard and a slightly more spacious back garden that had sprung up around the planned core of the city in the decades surrounding World War II.

Like so many other men—those brought in by fathers, uncles, older brothers, and other family members who had also worked at the plant in the years since its opening in 1941—Tom Hazel spent decades earning his daily bread at the foundry. It provided employment to close to one thousand of the area's residents and produced some of the purest aluminum in the world. True, the work was debilitating, but the financial compensations were good. Workers knew they would earn enough to be able to send their kids to college, pay off their mortgages, travel a little bit, and put aside some money for down the road. They also knew they'd be able to quit working while still young enough to enjoy spending those painstakingly accumulated nest eggs. For Tom, that was one of the main reasons he stayed at the job those many years.

Under contract provisions negotiated by the United Steel Workers and the factory's longtime parent company, Reynolds, the aluminum workers had the right to retire at a full pension after thirty years and receive $37.25 per month for every year of employment. It wasn't going to make anyone rich, but with Social Security added in it was enough to keep a man and his family out of poverty. Moreover, under a complex provision designed to protect young employees who burnt out early from the exhausting and dangerous physical labor, the Reynolds staff had the right to retire at a partial pension after twenty years, so long as the number of years they'd worked plus the number of years old they were combined to at least sixty-five. That was important; for while a white-collar worker might stay physically healthy into their fifties or sixties, the aluminum factory workers—repeatedly lifting heavy weights, breathing in toxic fumes, and risking burns, broken bones, even death among the vats of molten ore—generally were bedeviled by a host of health ailments by the time they settled into middle age.

On a good day, working conditions at the aluminum plant were just unpleasant. When things went wrong, they became extremely dangerous. Temperatures in the foundry soared well past one hundred degrees; the respirator masks the workers wore (and often tore holes in, they would recall with machismo gusto, to be able to smoke cigarettes) limited, but didn't entirely prevent, toxins from entering their lungs; and the lugging of aluminum studs and seventy-pound wrenches was often backbreaking work. There had been a handful of fatalities over the past several decades, including a man cut in half by falling equipment, two men burned to death by molten metal, and one man electrocuted. Of all the ways to die, the slow death of a mortally burned victim, the skin destroyed by liquid metal, the organs—rendered useless by the toxins—seizing up, has to be among the very worst. And then there were the long-term affects, the ones you couldn't see before they hit you and your buddies but which hurt just as much as hot spilt ore: veterans of the industry were known to be particularly prone to leukemia and a host of lung diseases.

"I don't know how many times I thought about quitting," one of Hazel's colleagues admitted, slightly sheepish, perhaps ashamed at showing any signs of weakness. "But I thought, 'Boy, I've got too many years invested here. I can't afford to give up those years.' So I hung in with the aluminum industry, knowing I had benefits and retirement coming, a safety net beneath me."

When Reynolds was bought out by the world's largest aluminum company, Alcoa—which was looking for investments that could shore up that prestigious "largest in the world" status—the contract provisions stayed in place. In an era of growing uncertainty for America's industrial workforce, the Alcoa workers seemed to have a relatively sweet future. Even if Alcoa shut the plant down, the company itself—*Alcoa, for Pete's sake*—wasn't about to go bankrupt, which meant that the workers' pensions were secure.

Hazel, who had a pension coming his way of about one thousand dollars a month, plus the Social Security that would kick in when he was sixty-two, had modest expectations for his golden years. "I would have had my thirty years in when I was fifty," he explained. "I would have maybe worked part time somewhere, moved up to Hook Canal or the coast. I like clamming and crabbing and getting oysters. You just walk right out on the beach and pick 'em up, take out your boats and drop your crab pots. I expected I'd be comfortable with my retirement, and my medical, and my savings."

Then, disaster struck.

In the early 2000s, energy prices, especially in the western United States, soared, and aluminum plants in the northwest, plants that used a staggering amount of electricity, suddenly were a whole lot less profitable. Alcoa, which had already realized that the plant's old, polluting technology and aging workforce were going to be drags on company profits, started looking around for a way to get out of its recent purchase. It turned to a venture capitalist from Chicago, Michael Lynch, a man who had earlier tried to purchase the facility and who had a track record of buying good metal-producing companies, letting them slide into bankruptcy, and then essentially selling them off for parts.

Back in 2000 Lynch had offered to put up $150 million. But Alcoa, perhaps fearing he couldn't actually pony up the cash that he was promising, had pooh-poohed the offer. Alcoa didn't exactly turn Lynch down, but it did put the negotiations into a holding pattern. Now, though, things were very different. In 2001, the Enron-manufactured energy crisis hit the western states, with large electricity-supply companies creating artificial power shortages as a way to drive up the price of their product. Starved of access to electricity, utility companies couldn't meet their customers' demands. And so, to prevent the grid going down, they began offering large-scale users huge rebates if they would temporarily shut down their facilities.

Like other foundries in the area, Longview, which had its own on-site electricity substation, had contracts with the local utility company, BPA, guaranteeing it access to stupendous amounts of energy. The electricity was needed to separate the oxygen in the ore from the metal in the hundreds of "pots" within the plant. That fall, BPA informed Alcoa that it would give the company $266 million if it would temporarily cease operations. It was an unbelievable amount of money, many times the value of the plant's annual aluminum output.

Alcoa leapt at the offer. *Who wouldn't have?* Enter Lynch again. The Chicagoan informed BPA that it couldn't close the deal with Alcoa since he had already bid on the plant, and Alcoa didn't have the right to shut down what might soon be a factory belonging to someone else. Faced with Lynch's legal stalling tactics, and needing to recoup the factory's electricity immediately, BPA offered a compromise: Alcoa would sell to Lynch; Lynch, who had had trouble raising the $150 million needed to buy the plant, would borrow from a bank that would in turn have the money repaid it in full by BPA; and, in installments, the more than $100 million that remained of the energy deal money would be paid out after Lynch shut down his newly acquired factory. In essence, the utility company was funding the purchase of a large customer so as to take that customer out of operation.

Given the circumstances, it was a win-win situation for all parties . . . except Longview's workers.

Under the terms of the contract, Alcoa was still responsible for the workers' pensions once they turned sixty-two. Now it was Michael Lynch, however, rather than Alcoa, who was the guarantor of their pensions between the time they retired and the time they reached sixty-two—which, for most workers, would be at least a decade. Moreover, if Lynch allowed the site to go bankrupt, workers like Hazel, with almost thirty years behind them, would be unable to retire under the earlier provisions. And the icing on the cake: all of the workers would immediately lose their health benefits.

To no one's surprise, that was exactly what happened. Lynch closed the plant down, as agreed upon with BPA; and, despite a smoke-and-mirrors game that lasted into 2003, it never reopened. That year, Longview Aluminum officially declared bankruptcy, owing Cowlitz County $2 million in unpaid taxes and skipping out on the tens of millions of dollars in pensions obligations to its employees.

And so, less than six months before Tom Hazel's thirty-year anniversary rolled around, he found himself locked out of the pension system for the next twelve years. Even worse, his medical benefits, which, under the union contract, were supposed to last the rest of his life, were cancelled.

Faced with impending personal bankruptcy, Hazel had to virtually empty the small 401(k) he had built up during his years of employment to keep his wife, his young son, and a grandson whom he had officially gained guardianship over a few years earlier afloat. Bang went the dreams of clamming and the early morning walks on the seafront. Bang went the notion of slowing down after three decades of punching in on the factory time cards. After thirty years of turning ore into metal, Tom Hazel found himself on the job market once more, a middle-aged man competing with hundreds of other newly unemployed men in a town that had just had its economic heart ripped out.

Hazel's story, and that of the countless other employees of the Longview Aluminum plant, was just one saga within an unfolding national crisis. During the Bush years, large corporate employers, fearful of their growing financial obligations to an aging workforce, stampeded away from their pension obligations, some by selling parts of themselves off to predatory venture capitalists, others by either declaring bankruptcy or simply threatening to declare bankruptcy unless courts allowed them to downsize their pension pledges. And, in an era in which workplace rights were being eroded at a startling pace, the courts were only too happy to oblige. The result was that for all too many American workers, the pensions guaranteed them by union-negotiated contracts literally vanished. They were victims of a conservative, anti–trade union political climate that tolerated brazen rollbacks of benefits packages established over decades, and allowed private companies to shed their pensions, secure in the knowledge that the Pension Benefits Guarantee Corporation (PBGC)—an obscure branch of the federal government created in 1974 and funded by insurance premiums paid into it by private companies—would step in with partial compensation to the workers.

In the early years of this century, employees at some of America's largest, most respected corporations saw their guaranteed pensions slashed and their promised health-care coverage entirely disappear. Among the biggest offenders were United Air Lines, Delta Airlines, and Bethlehem Steel.

In late 2002, as Bethlehem Steel teetered on the edge of insolvency, the PBGC took over its pension plan. The plan covered nearly 100,000 workers, but the steel behemoth had underfunded it to the tune of $4.3 billion. A couple years later, in early 2005, a bankrupt United Air Lines dumped 120,000 current and future pensions onto the government. The International Association of Machinists and Aerospace Workers estimated benefits for its members would be slashed by up to 27 percent. Flight attendants faced even steeper cuts. In September 2005, Delta also filed for bankruptcy. The company emerged from it after two years with 20 percent less staff and having transferred the responsibility for the pensions of its thirteen thousand pilots onto the PBGC. In December 2006, as they were hammering out the final details of the pension termination—which meant that most of the pilots would see sizeable reductions in their benefits—U.S. bankruptcy judge Adlai Hardin called the settlement "eminently reasonable."

Increasingly, the large automakers and auto-parts companies, their profits hobbled by high pension and medical coverage costs, as well as by plummeting sales, were also making noises about rolling back their pensions. When the large auto-parts maker Delphi filed for bankruptcy in 2005, GM picked up the tab for much of its pension obligations. As a result, by October 2005 Ron Tadross, a Bank of America securities analyst, was estimating that each GM share carried with it six dollars in pension liabilities. Several industry analysts declared it was only a matter of time before the auto giant sought bankruptcy protection. It didn't—but it did freeze its traditional pension benefits, replacing them instead with a 401(k) system. Then it began cutting health benefits for retirees. And finally it stopped making matching contributions into employees' 401(k) accounts.

As the economy worsened in 2008, the doom-and-gloom drumbeat intensified. By September, rumors abounded regarding an impending declaration of bankruptcy by General Motors. And by October its share price was down around the five dollar mark—meaning each share was worth less than the pension liabilities attached to it. The company denied it would seek Chapter 11 protections, but not all analysts were convinced. There was, predicted New York University business professor Edward Altman, a 50 percent chance of the auto giant going into bankruptcy. By November, the talk was not just of GM going bankrupt, but of all three of Detroit's major auto companies biting the dust. And by December, with a congressional bailout of the auto industry in doubt, there was talk that two of the big three would not survive far into 2009. Were such a seismic event to transpire in the coming years, in addition to the cascading unemployment that would ensue, hundreds of thousands of retirees and their families would likely see their benefits cut.

Elsewhere, company towns such as Kannapolis, North Carolina, home to the Pillowtex Corporation textile company, and northern Minnesota communities like Hoytlake, reliant on jobs provided by LTV Steel, saw their one major industry go bottom up and their senior citizens' pensions collapse with it. In Kannapolis alone, that meant many thousands of private pensions simply crumbled into dust. In Elmwood, New Jersey, Marcal Paper Mills went the way of the dodo, and its retirees started receiving monthly checks from the PBGC.

When the LTV Steel company plant in Cleveland, Ohio, shut down after the company went bankrupt in 2001, many local retirees saw their pension benefits halved. In September 2008, Brian Albrecht, a reporter for the Cleveland *Plain Dealer*, profiled one such man who had had to come out of retirement to work a low-wage job taking telephone reservations for a hotel chain.

Between 2002 and 2006, the number of monthly pensions being paid out by the PBGC almost doubled. By 2008, nearly 700,000 Americans relied on the federal government to pay private pensions that had been promised them by their employers; hundreds of thousands more workers would end up on the PBGC rolls once they hit retirement age. And all indications were that many more large-scale private pension programs would similarly disintegrate in the coming years. As a result of this trend, the PBGC went far into the red. In 2000, the corporation was running a billion-dollar surplus. Six years later, it had a deficit approaching $25 billion. Nine of the ten biggest pension defaults in American history had occurred during this six-year period, and across America experts calculated that companies had underfunded their pension plans to the tune of hundreds of billions of dollars, most of that underfunding having occurred between 2002 and 2004.

When George Bush was elected president in 2000, employer-funded pensions were short about $30 billion. Four years later, that deficit was up to nearly half a trillion, with some estimates putting the final tally at closer to double that. At least $100 billion of this shortfall could be traced to companies that investment experts believed likely to fail in the not too distant future. Even more worryingly, according to the analysts at Mercer's International Retirement Specialty Group, if the stock market collapse of the autumn of 2008 wasn't quickly reversed, the fifteen hundred largest publicly traded companies in America would likely face pension fund deficits of $400 billion in the years ahead.

These numbers were staggering in their enormity. Quite simply, companies were making promises they either couldn't keep or simply had no intention of keeping, and government regulatory agencies were standing back and letting the game of illusions continue.

In the two years following 2006, the administration finally awoke to the scale of the problem and began, halfheartedly, pushing for reforms and raising the insurance premiums it charged participating companies. The PBGC's deficit fell considerably—but in large part that was due to a temporarily surging stock market. Close to 40 percent of the PBGC's approximately $60 billion in assets were invested in equity, up from only a quarter a few years earlier; and in 2008 the rules were further relaxed, allowing for 45 percent to be so invested. On paper, at least, the corporation was doing very well. By 2008 its deficit was "only" $13 billion and its executives were predicting this would decline to $10 billion or less within a few years.

But as the stock market collapsed in September 2008, the long-term outlook for the corporation similarly fell—this at the very moment the threat of a serious recession meant that more companies would likely start defaulting on their pension obligations over the coming years. Like Fannie Mae and Freddie Mac, PBGC wasn't investing conservatively. "The new allocation will likely also carry more risk than acknowledged by PBGC's analysis," researchers at the Government Accountability Office (GAO) warned a few months before the market tanked. "The agency faces unique challenges." Sure enough, a month later the head of PBGC testified before the House Committee on Education and Labor. Due to the recent market turmoil, he informed the politicians, the PBGC expected the value of its assets to decline by about 7 percent in 2008.

There were, in many ways, stark similarities between the country's failing pension system and the resulting demands being placed on the federal government, and the savings and loans debacle of the 1980s as well as the subprime crisis two decades later. All were products of casino capitalism, based on the faulty assumption that you could continually bet against the house and always end up a winner.

When Fannie Mae and Freddie Mac toppled, and the federal government had to pump trillions of dollars into a slew of financial rescue packages, the government assumed a whole new level of bailout burden. Here, too, the government had stood back and watched— or actively undermined legislative safeguards designed to protect against meltdown—while large companies took their investors' and employees' money and, in the name of quick-turnaround profits, headed toward quicksand. Now the GAO was saying that the pension insurance system, already inadequate and unable to fully make up for the value of lost private pensions and benefits, could see a similar tale of woe unfold.

Whether the story was pension systems in crisis or mortgage lenders in collapse, the underlying narrative of these years was one of risk transferal: private companies were being encouraged to take extraordinary risks and were being permitted to fall back on the government for help when their risks didn't pan out or their contractual obligations proved more costly than they had originally anticipated. The language that was used belonged to the free market, but in reality this was anything but true laissez-faire economics. Rather, it was about sticking taxpayers and retirees with the bill when the times got tough for large corporations. Time after time during the Bush years, whenever the deregulation philosophy broke down, it was followed by emergency responses, improvised and extraordinarily costly government interventions, and market chaos.

In the same way as Wal-Mart was getting away with underpaying its workers and providing shamefully inadequate health-care benefits, secure in the knowledge that government programs such as food stamps and heating assistance would provide much-needed subsidies, companies like United Air Lines and Bethlehem Steel were failing to put enough money aside for their pensions. They knew that when push came to shove the PBGC would ride to the rescue. And while leading Democrats, such as ex-Senator John Edwards, had long pushed for a reform of the bankruptcy process that better protected workers' pensions and prevented the executives of bankrupt companies from walking away with multimillion-dollar handouts, the Bush White House wasn't interested in such safeguards. When the four-hundred-page Pension Protection Act of 2006 was passed, companies that went into bankruptcy were forced to pay a modest surcharge to the PBGC for each worker whose pension they cancelled; but the pensions themselves weren't really shored up. In fact, in many ways the legislation's authors chose to simply scale back workers' expectations rather than force companies to meet their contractual obligations: Companies were given seven years to rectify the underfunding of their pension plans; in the meantime, the Act limited the benefit increases that companies could allocate to their employees.

At the same time, as corporations responded to signals from the administration that Washington was no longer in the business of protecting private pensions, more and more companies, including IBM, DuPont, and several other blue chip institutions, replaced defined-benefit pensions with riskier 401(k) plans, froze the contributions they were making into the 401(k)s, or simply cut back the benefits that they provided retirees. During his campaign for the Democratic Party's presidential nomination, John Edwards claimed that from 2005 through early 2008 nearly two-thirds of U.S. companies had frozen their pension plans, and one in five workers had actually seen reductions in the size of their eventual retirement benefits. This trend was a startling reversal of three quarters of a century of government policy aimed to shore up and protect the nation's pension systems.

The two main problems associated with the Bush model were that 1) government agencies ultimately responsible for the bailouts were themselves underfunded, viable only if they were rarely utilized, and 2) individual workers and taxpayers got hammered in the process—through denuded pensions and benefits as well as the accumulation of mountains of new government debt that, eventually, would have to be paid off via tax revenues.

The collapse of private pension plans has meant the end not only of workers' expectations of a financially secure old age, but also, and just as important, the health insurance that stands between illness and destitution. For many thousands of these men and women, too young for Medicare, too sick to be able to buy into private insurance systems—even if they had the money to do so—this transformation spells pure ruin. While the PBGC pays full pensions up to a fairly generous maximum for employees who work until they are at least sixty-two years old, for those who have retired early, or who planned to, the pensions paid by the corporation are miniscule. Moreover, the PBGC does not cover health insurance when it crafts bailouts for floundering private pension systems.

"It's a frightful societal development. When they [the companies] go bankrupt, they take good union-paying jobs out of the economy, which are hard to replace," stated Bill Brandt, who worked for the Chicago-based company Development Specialists, Inc. and served as a trustee during the Chapter 11 bankruptcy proceedings of some of these businesses. "Your medical benefits have been horribly compromised as well. Thirdly, when you finally get to retirement you discover that which was promised you for retirement has also been horribly compromised. You're inventory dating for poverty. They know it's coming. It's just a matter of when." For upper-middle-aged workers like Hazel, Brandt was extremely pessimistic. "They will discover it's the beginning of a very sordid story for the rest of their lives, where the promises made to them will not be kept."

Nationally, Second Harvest estimated that it was feeding 3 million seniors by 2008. The Census Bureau calculated that close to 10 percent of the country's elderly population was living below the poverty line. As pension systems collapsed, and as privately held IRAs declined in value with the intensification of the economic crisis, those numbers looked likely to increase. The careful calculations upon which so many millions had prepared for their golden years suddenly no longer held true.

In western Washington State, of which Longview is a part, Food Lifeline reported that 13 percent of the people using food banks and meal programs in 2008 were seniors. Many more were at the high end of middle age, people, like Hazel, who were not old enough to qualify for Social Security and yet were no longer drawing good paychecks from career jobs.

By 2008, in addition to the lost jobs and pensions at the aluminum plant, Longview was hemorrhaging employment across the board. A local fiber plant was laying off workers; Weyerhauser mills was slimming down; Steelscape was sending out pink slips. "What we've been seeing is a steady loss of jobs," said Alan Rose, the Development and Community Relations Director for the Lower Columbia Community Action Program, a week before Christmas. "My agency is the food distribution center for the eight [local] food banks. We've seen an 8 percent increase from this time last year. We're seeing a lot more of the working poor. The middle-aged. Younger people who have a job and still are not able to make ends meet." The agency was also, he noted, having to help "people who've lost their pensions or had their pensions reduced. They'd turn up more in the emergency food assistance program."

As elsewhere in the country, large numbers of the region's hungry reported having to choose between buying food or paying for rent, heating, and medical care.

In late 2008, Food Lifeline estimated the number of meals low-income residents of Cowlitz County could provide for themselves, received from public assistance programs, or were given via hunger-relief groups. They then worked out the percentage of meals still missing. *The result?* There was a shortfall of 1.3 million meals per year, or nearly 5 percent of the total meals needed by impoverished locals. Put another way, on average, a low-income resident of the country was missing meals at least once a week during the course of a year. Shockingly, throughout much of Washington State the shortfall was even more pronounced.

Cowlitz County, of which Longview was the county seat, had one food bank in 2001; seven years later, it had eight, and they were still struggling to keep up with the growing demand. By the end of 2008, reported Camille Wells, public relations manager for Food Lifeline, the number of seniors using the services had risen sharply. "For people living on a fixed income, when there's an economic crisis there are things that aren't normally budgeted for. And food is usually the first thing to be cut from the budget. We've reported up to about one-third of the people who've come into food banks this calendar year have never been to food banks before. The situation of the economy has driven that many more people to emergency food. It's pushing our agencies to the limits. It's been the busiest in the thirty years we've been in business."

While the food banks didn't track the detailed employment histories of their clients, it was a fair bet that, as the broader economy worsened, many of Longview's laid-off aluminum workers—especially those nearing, or at, retirement age—were now showing up on the region's growing breadlines.

The day the Longview aluminum plant died, many of the old-timers went down to Grumpy's Tavern and proceeded to get as drunk as humanly possible. It seemed the only sensible response to the collapse of their retirement dreams. "It was a really hurtful time," recalled one of the men, Ken Williams, a Vietnam vet, who was fifty-four years old when the bankruptcy was announced. His retirement date had been set for a mere three months later.

Williams, a smartly dressed man, his balding head shaved, a white walrus mustache adorning his tanned face, looked somewhat like the 1970s TV personality Kojak. When I met him three years later, he was working for a local realty holding company as a handyman, earning about a third what he earned at the aluminum plant. "I was just hoping, 'Get me them few more days here. That's all I'm asking.' I'd get my pension plus four hundred dollars a month [another contract provision relating to the closing down of the plant] till I got my Social Security. I felt totally shafted. You were just kind of stunned, you know. All them years you'd worked toward something and gave yourself to a company. I felt terrible. It ain't fair."

"I was six months from retirement," Hazel explained, a bemused, almost resigned tone to his voice. "It's sitting there waiting for me, and I don't know if in ten years Alcoa will be there to give it to me, or if it is around they will give it to me. The worst thing was not knowing I had a guaranteed future; that all I'd worked for was gone; and I didn't know what was to come. I knew people living in vans and cars. It scared me; not having a house and not being able to take care of my kids."

One of Hazel's colleagues, an African American named Bernie

King, was a devoutly religious man in his mid-fifties. He cycled into depression and, eventually, homelessness, for close to a year. He ended up living out of his van, sleeping in mall parking lots, and using Burger King bathrooms to try to wash himself and go to the toilet. Another, Wes Wheeler, retrained as a pharmacist's assistant and counted himself lucky to have landed a job at Wal-Mart, a job that paid less than half what he used to earn and came with virtually no benefits. He got health care through his wife's job, but once she retired the couple would lose all their medical coverage. "Earning half of what I used to make," Wheeler recalled, "in a way I felt fortunate, because there were a lot of people not getting work at the time. I'll never make the big money I was making at the plant, and I realize that and have adjusted my life accordingly. I don't buy new cars, have things that need to be done to my house. You have to be on top of your finances all the time, because I have nothing to fall back on." Several of Wheeler's friends let the tension destroy their family lives, and spiraled into divorce and alcoholism. One killed himself, and another went insane.

"I felt betrayed," said fifty-nine-year-old Eugene Murphy, a feisty man who grew up on a farm in Minnesota. He was wearing a yellow baseball cap, a black T-shirt, and jeans, and was chewing a sausage, egg, and cheese croissant as we talked. "I feel betrayed by the whole country, that they let the aluminum industry collapse. There's not hardly a drop of aluminum produced anymore in the northwest, and we used to be a powerhouse." Three years on, Murphy, who did a stint driving a combine on a pea farm after the plant shut, was working as a security guard, earning half what he used to earn and, when he got sick, having to drive twenty miles each way to the one doctor in the region whom he was allowed to see under his employer's limited health insurance plan. His friend Bill Hannah had also been hired on as a guard, working for the Department of Homeland Security at the Port of Longview. He earned $9.15 an hour and had to pay $524 per month for catastrophic health insurance for himself and his wife.

For Dan Fowler, fifty-three years old, divorced, and bedeviled by health problems, the plant's closure and the end of his insurance coverage through Kaiser Permanente meant he now had to go down to Longview's family health clinic to get free medical care. The waits were long, the service somewhat rudimentary. When he needed medications for high blood pressure and high cholesterol, or when he had to restock on Albuterol for the inhaler he used for his weak lungs, he was reduced to pleading for free samples from the clinic. "If they didn't give me samples all the time, I'd be looking at two hundred dollars a month at the very least." When he had to have four cancerous lesions removed from his face, it cost him thousands of dollars—bills he could only pay by cashing in his meager 401(k). When he had a scare, a couple years after the plant closed, over a possible brain tumor, he struggled to get the tests he needed because the providers demanded cash up front.

Tom Hazel managed to get his kids enrolled in a state-funded health insurance program. But he had to start paying a hefty monthly premium for his wife and himself. As the bills mounted, he had no choice but to raid his 401(k), taking out $40,000 of the $50,000 he'd managed to put away as a nest egg for his old age.

More than a year after the plant permanently shut its doors, Hazel—one of the relatively lucky ones among the middle-aged men in his cohort at the plant—got a job driving a forklift at another local mill, a timber plant owned by Weyerhauser. After taxes, he was now earning about one thousand dollars every two weeks, far less than the income he'd built up to at the aluminum company with nearly three decades of seniority under his belt. Instead of spending his fifties clamming and fishing for oysters up the Washington coast, he would be driving a forklift, struggling to stay above water and pay off the debts he accumulated when he lost his job, struggling to make good his shattered expectations.

"It really tears your future up. I was angry at everybody. It pissed you off they'd do that to you that easily. You're like a checkmark in a book. They checked you off, after you helped them make the money they made."

"When I was working at Reynolds," Hazel's erstwhile colleague Wheeler recalled, more wistful than furious, "I just thought I'd put my time in, retire, and be taken care of. The big thing is medical. Me working in the pharmacy, I see it all the time, people coming in trying to work out whether to buy medications or put food on the table. Hopefully, I won't be in that situation. I'll save my nickels, and hopefully I can afford to buy insurance when I retire, or else continue to work until I can't work anymore."

■ ■ ■

Interlude V

The only thing that troubled me a little, in spite
of the nausea that the thought of food inspired in
me, was hunger. I commenced to be sensible of a
shameless appetite again; a ravenous lust of food,
which grew steadily worse and worse. It gnawed
unmercifully at my breast; carrying on a silent,
mysterious work in there.

—Knut Hamsun, *Hunger* (1890)

When you're hungry, you get irritable easily. And one of the surefire shortcuts to irritability is the knowledge that the only food you can afford is the kind of joyless fare you eat simply to survive.

I dumped my knotted green plastic bags from the food pantry down on my kitchen floor and ripped them open. There was a lot of food, but not a whole lot of coherence binding the selection; in fact, in its randomness, my collection of items looked like it was the end result of a child being let loose in a supermarket. More serious, as I had feared would be the case, half of it was of the ingest-at-your-own-risk variety. Were I literally starving, I would have eaten it without a second thought; being merely hungry, my desire to avoid making myself sick triumphed. As many other food pantry clients had told me they did, I began to categorize my food into piles: *edible and useful*, *edible but useless*, and *inedible: to be immediately thrown away*.

To be immediately thrown away: bread eight days past its sell-by date; a huge bag of old, rock-hard bread rolls; a slimy thirty-two-ounce carton of plain yogurt, so far beyond its use-by date that I was scared to even open it; a dented small bottle of ancient Gatorade; a keep-frozen chicken stew, past its sell-by date and obviously long unfrozen; a jar of dusty old Manischewitz gefilte fish (clearly my "shopper" at the food bank had done what I did when a volunteer: she had tried to personalize my pantry experience, had looked at my last name, assumed, rightly, that I was Jewish, and then assumed, wrongly, that therefore I liked gefilte fish. As it happens, it is one of the few foods on earth that literally makes me gag).

To be put aside for further investigation: two bags of stuck-together old Danish pastries and bagels, the sugary icing practically fermenting inside the sweaty sacks. (Ultimately, I nibbled on a few of the soggy Danishes and determined they were nasty enough to merit immediate removal.) And three cartons of Mexican molé sauce—which would have been wonderful if I had had a chicken, or indeed any sort of meat, on which to pour them.

To be kept for sustenance: three bags of extremely old pita bread, with a sell-by date four months past, that must have come out of a restaurant deep freeze and, therefore, could not be refrozen. I'd eat the pita bread until it either moldered or became too stale to bear. A big bag of sugar-coated Hershey's Chocolate Kisses. One portion of ravioli, only two days past use-by—a treasure that would provide me dinner on my first night. A bag of white rice. One can of split pea soup. A can of olives, one of corn, another of low-end tomato sauce, one of creamed corn, and a can of USDA-issued kidney beans. I had one box of instant mac 'n' cheese, three packets of ramen noodles, one Rice-A-Roni, a bag of macaroni pasta, and two single-portion pack-ets of oatmeal. There was enough food, if used sparingly, to keep me going for about five days, and possibly another day or two past that.

To be wished for but not present: meat, fish, edible dairy products of any sort, fresh vegetables, fruit (either of the fresh or canned vari-ety), juice, eggs, cooking oil, or spices.

I wasn't going to starve, but I wasn't going to be eating healthily either. Lots of starch and sugar, a paucity of vitamins and protein. And I knew, from my earlier experiences, that my body would rapidly start demanding compensation for what it lacked. *Sure, I'll let you feed me with crap*, my stomach would warn me, *but you're going to have to stuff an awful lot of that crap into me so I can extract what little protein and vitamins I can from the noodles and rice and salty ramen and canned beans. You're going to have to stuff in handfuls of Hershey's Kisses every few hours so I can pretend all that sugar energy is good energy.* In fact, for the few days I was living on a food pantry diet, I might actually eat more, in sheer food weight, than I usually did at each meal, and I might cram in handfuls of sweets and plates full of pita bread in between those meals; but I wouldn't feel full and I'd speedily run low on pep.

My nutritional adviser, Amy Block Joy, emailed me that I would be fine for a few days. But if a poor person were to come to rely primarily on these sorts of food handouts, stretching them to cover perhaps two weeks out of the month, as many food pantry recipients were doing by the grim autumn of 2008, they would start to undermine their health over a period of months. "Unless the person is already low in vitamins," Block wrote, "they will not show deficiencies or have clinical significance for many weeks, maybe months on this diet. The major concern would be calcium, which is found in milk and milk products, although, again, there is some in beans. Calcium is needed for bone density, so the effects on women would be more than on men and the problems would not occur until women are much older [osteoporosis]. However, pregnant women would not do well on this diet due to the needs of the developing baby. Children also would suffer consequences."

In other words, even though I, as a healthy, middle-class, still-youngish man, would likely get miserable and lethargic eating such poor fare, once I came off the diet I'd bounce back pretty quickly; others wouldn't be so lucky. "One other issue," Joy warned, "is the diet is poor so that the body's immune system would be less than perfect and perhaps many might suffer from respiratory colds, developing flu or, worse, pneumonia."

Over the next few days, I lived mainly on what I'd been given. I added in a little bit of cooking oil, a pat of butter for the pita bread, coffee, and the milk and sugar to go in it. When I made the oatmeal, I just stirred it up with water. When I cooked the pasta, I put a few tinned olives into the watery tomato sauce; corn with pasta seemed too strange, so I simply ate half a can by itself.

There's not much to tell about a low-protein, low-vitamin diet like this. You don't lose weight—if anything, fairly quickly you would start to put on pounds—and Professor Joy was probably right that clinically there was nothing too damaging about it. But that gnawing feeling never really left my stomach. Pita bread was good for soaking up the acid; ten or twenty Hershey's kisses would give me a shot of energy good for maybe half an hour; the low-grade pasta temporarily filled me up but a few minutes later I'd need to snack again.

Like Aubretia Edick, I drank a lot of hot tea, and also coffee, to warm me up. It wasn't cold outside, but by the evening of day two my body felt chronically under the weather; nothing too serious, just a continual feeling of mild malaise. I craved the salt from the ramen noodles, but after I ate a bowl of it I'd still be just as hungry as I'd been before my meal. By the end of day three, no matter how much starch and salt and sugar I stuffed into my mouth, my stomach answered *more*.

I was eating too much of the wrong sorts of food and none of the right kinds of food. I was binging when the food was in front of me and miserable when it wasn't. I had become that strange specimen, a hungry person with an abundance of starch on my hands. I had become a hungry American.

SIX
—

Grapes of Wrath Regurgitated

> There has been no war in California, no plague, no bombing of open towns and roads, no shelling of cities. It is a beautiful year. And thousands of families are starving in California . . . It is to the advantage of the corporate farmer to have too much labor, for then wages can be cut. Then people who are hungry will fight each other for a job rather than the employer for a living wage.
>
> —John Steinbeck, "Starvation Under the Orange Trees" (*Monterey Trader*, April 15, 1938)

THREE-QUARTERS OF A CENTURY AGO, the plains rebelled. Not the people, but the ground itself. Overused farmland in the middle of the country literally turned to dust, its broken topsoil swirling over town and countryside alike in vast and deadly dust storms. Grainy black-and-white images from those days look truly apocalyptic. The dense clouds of pulverized earth descended with the force of hurricanes, leaving houses buried up to the second floor, tractors trapped in fields with only their seats and steering wheels left visible. In towns like Boise City, in the far western corner of Oklahoma, residents hid in their homes, their windows closed, wet cloths over their faces, waiting for the dust to depart, for the chance to dig their possessions out of the sand. In the space of a few years one of the world's great breadbaskets became a desert, a "dust bowl." And its population—the descendants of sodbusters who had, not too many years before, shoveled holes in the earth and made temporary, and tiny, subterranean "dugout" homes for their families while they tamed the land—began to starve. Entire families subsisted on roadkill and boiled tumbleweed. Food pantries in even the smallest towns were inundated with hundreds of desperate, gaunt supplicants. The journalist Timothy Egan, in his book *The Worst Hard Time*, wrote about the soup kitchen operated out of a sanatorium in the little town of Dalhart, Texas. "Some days, two hundred people waited in line: Mexicans who lived in the shanties near the Rock Island roundhouse, drifters who had just stepped off the train, and longtime Dalhart residents who had not seen a paycheck in three years."

The meager bowls of food people ate during those years, sang Woody Guthrie, the mournful folk music balladeer from Okemah, Oklahoma, in *Talking Dust Bowl Blues*, were "mighty thin stew, you could read a magazine right through it . . . if it had been just a little bit thinner some of these here politicians could have seen through it." In *Blowin' Down the Road* he sang of the farmer's hungry children and his refusal to accept his impoverished lot any longer.

The epicenter of the disaster was western Oklahoma, the Texas panhandle, and counties in eastern New Mexico. More than a century earlier, pioneers had pulled their wagons over this harsh landscape, navigating the famous Santa Fe Trail into terra incognita. When the earth crumbled in the 1930s, rutted wagon tracks were still visible from the air, ghostly reminders of the rush west two generations before the Civil War. (So, too, in places, were fossilized dinosaur footprints; over the decades, huge numbers of dinosaur fossils have been excavated from the dry lands of western Oklahoma.)

Fast forward to the present day, and the landscape of the Dust Bowl still remains, a monument to hubris frozen in time. These days, with a years-long drought drying up the land once again, you don't have to drive too far down country lanes off the main roads to see rotting wooden windmills and rusted tractor corpses poking up out of the sand piles that ruined the farmers of the 1930s, led to an epidemic of banks foreclosing on devalued properties, and sent thousands of destitute "Okies" westward. People and their possessions crammed into patched-up old cars and trucks, heading for the shantytowns and fields of central California.

Owing to an aggressive, government-mandated soil restoration program, the land gradually recovered. Those who hadn't fled tilled the soil once again. Cattle returned, too. Sparkling new grain silos were built. And prosperity, some of it agricultural, some reliant on the region's abundance of oil and natural gas, some revolving around military bases and high-tech centers, blossomed. In the post–World War II decades, small towns like Guymon, Oklahoma (population: 10,400), and the slightly larger city of Clovis, New Mexico, thrived; so, too, did the regional hub, the windswept Texas panhandle city of Amarillo, to whose railway yards cattle were driven before being transported north to the country's great slaughterhouses. With gasoline and diesel cheap and plentiful, farmers didn't think twice about driving an hour or more into town to go shopping or seek out entertainment. Supermarkets sprang up; then the all-in-one megastores. Small local grocers, hardware stores, and clothing shops went out of business in many hamlets. Increasingly, the Main Streets of smaller communities were abandoned; shop windows were broken or boarded up, the paint on the old buildings left to peel off. Perversely, their desolation was, at first, almost seen as a badge of wealth, a symbol of a mobile moment when even the lowliest farmworker owned a car and could afford to make the long drive into town whenever he felt like spending a few dollars.

In Melrose, New Mexico (population: 750), a one-traffic-light town similar to so many others on the Great Plains, sun-bronzed farmers hunched over instant coffees at the gas station diner next to the tire repair shop. Elderly men and women trooped into the senior center, fronting onto Main Street, for their quilting clubs and free lunches. The school perched on the town limits gave out more and more subsidized meals, and the shortfall was made up by a newly opened pantry. Bar a couple banks and thrift stores, the businesses that had once helped build the town were gone, replaced by bigger stores in bigger towns stretched along the highways and state routes of the region.

"People used to go everywhere. We're used to going one hundred miles to go somewhere," explained local farmer Don Smith. "Lubbock's one hundred twenty-five miles. Amarillo, one hundred fifty. Roswell's at least one hundred." Smith was a large man who had lost his right arm in a farming accident back when he was a child. His injury didn't hold him back. He was, by 2008, one of the area's few remaining successful farmers, drove a huge pickup truck, and was as in love with the land as any man could be.

In the 1990s and 2000s, entire communities came to be referred to as "food deserts," places with nowhere to buy food within thirty or forty miles other than the small, overpriced convenience stores attached to gas stations. But none of this seemed to matter, or so the boosters kept saying; the bigger towns had the large stores, and those stores, Wal-Marts in particular, offered choices and prices that benefited everyone, whether they came from near or far.

The small-town children and grandchildren of the Dust Bowl survivors, men and women who commuted to work in the larger regional towns, stopped growing their own food and supporting their neighborhood businesses. "We had cattle and we grew the feed for our cattle," recalled sixty-eight-year-old Lynette Taylor nostalgically, over a coffee at one of Guymon's down-home diners. Taylor— a volunteer at the local food pantry—and her husband, Marvin, lived far out in the country, their nearest neighbors five miles away. They had farmed their 2,400 acres—land homesteaded by Marvin's grandparents in the early twentieth century, before Oklahoma was made a state in 1907—from their youth until the onset of old age, when her husband had a stroke and could no longer work. "We haven't even had any cattle in the last seven years. We may be going back to more of that, where we're more self-sufficient; have a calf to butcher, a pig to butcher, a little garden." But Taylor recognized the return to self-sufficiency wouldn't happen overnight. "The costs [of farming] are increasing. And people are leasing their land out to bigger corporations, bigger farmers. Our population is getting older. No new, young farmers are going into the business. They really can't afford to. And people don't want to work on the farm anymore."

Removed from the land, locals gradually lost the knowledge of how to survive independently, a knowledge that had seen genera-tions of pioneers, homesteaders, and Dust Bowl–era farmers in the region through bitterly hard times. And yet, they remained rural, dwellers on a vast land without the sort of food-distribution infra-structure present in larger, denser population hubs. They could get away with having big-city consumption habits only so long as jobs remained plentiful and gas for their vehicles cheap.

Unfortunately, prosperity was tenuous at best. And when it disap-peared, the food desert communities, along with the people living in them who no longer knew how to grow their own food, were left high and dry. "Ten or twenty years ago, everybody had a garden, cows, chickens, the whole nine yards," Smith recollected. Then, he continued, people got used to the convenience of driving to super-markets, and they stopped growing their own food. As a result, they left themselves peculiarly vulnerable to being hit by changes in the broader economy. "Now nobody's driving anywhere," he went on, "because gas is $3.79 a gallon."

Seeing his neighbors starting to go hungry, Smith convinced one of Melrose's local landowners to let him use a one-room shack backing onto the railway tracks (it was so close that the building vibrated whenever one of the mile-long freight trains rumbled past) and opened it up as a food pantry. Pulling favors, he got forty-pound blocks of cheese donated, convinced the local motorcycle club to rustle up five hundred dollars to buy canned produce from a regional food bank, and even had the grieving family of a lady recently deceased to ask mourners to donate to the pantry rather than buy flowers for the funeral. But all of that was stopgap stuff. As fast as the food came in, it got snapped up. Triggered by surging gas prices and then, more generally, by economic collapse, the hunger, it seemed, was unstoppable.

For Lynette and Marvin Taylor, the tipping point came when they were almost stranded in Arizona by the soaring gasoline prices. "When they started skyrocketing, we were out in Arizona. My sister was sick and we were taking care of her. When they skyrocketed, we still had to get home. Well, we made it home, but we haven't traveled much since then," said Lynette. Then they stopped driving into town except when it was absolutely necessary, and when they did come in they drove their five-year-old Ford Expedition slowly down the empty road to make their gas stretch just that little bit further. "I try to group things together so I can do them all at one time, get everything done. My husband's parents, they had a list, and if something needed to be done they'd put it on the list. That's kind of what we're back to. Particularly for rural people."

In Boise City, the rundown county seat for Cimarron County in the westernmost region of the state, things went from bad to cataclysmic. Farmers were being hammered by drought; the only new jobs were at a prison a couple towns over, or in a small cheese factory; and many businesses, including the town's one nursing home, had recently gone bottom up. Waitresses working Boise City's restaurants were paid two dollars an hour; like Idaho, Oklahoma exempted tipped employees from minimum-wage requirements. And even the good jobs—office work for the utility company or the county, clerkships at the courthouse—started out at seven or eight dollars an hour. Hardly anyone, it seemed, received health insurance through their work. Locals could buy food from a couple gas stations on the edge of town or from the lone, not particularly well-stocked grocery store on Main Street. If they could afford the gas, they could drive the better part of an hour to proper supermarkets in Guymon. Increasingly, however, that was not an option. By 2008, not far shy of half the town's thirteen hundred residents—and some of the food distribution volunteers believed even this was a conservative estimate—had been reduced to picking up charity eatables from the pantry, much of it trucked in from the regional food bank in Oklahoma City, hundreds of miles to the southeast.

"When I was a kid, we had two lumber companies, two grocery stores, a big motel, a shoe store, a clothing store," remembered fifty-six-year-old food pantry client Donna Stubblefield. Stubblefield was a large lady with purple fingernails, dyed ginger hair, and clothing that had clearly seen many, many better days. She lived in a mobile home and made her money babysitting local kids, but she rarely brought in more than three thousand dollars a year. "All of a sudden, we started losing things, and nothing was coming back. Now, we're at a standstill."

Although Mississippi regularly posts either the worst or second-worst hunger data in the country, in many ways that's an old story. The Delta has always had extremes of poverty and disempowerment—slaves, sharecroppers, tenant farmers on one side, estate owners on the other—much of it intertwined, historically, with its particularly ferocious race-based caste system. So, too, have the Carolinas, as well as the often-claustrophobic hills of Appalachia. These are regions that have, for generations, lagged behind much of the rest of the country in terms of economic progress. A United Nations Development Report released in 2008 estimated that residents of Kentucky's impoverished Fifth Congressional District had a life expectancy equal to that of the average American three decades earlier. The hungry in these parts today are the children, grandchildren, great-grandchildren of hungry Mississippians, Tennesseans,

Kentuckians, West Virginians. This doesn't, of course, negate the pain they feel—their hunger is no less real or tragic than that experienced elsewhere, in parts of America that either didn't develop in the shadow of endemic poverty or threw off the yoke of poverty decades ago—but it does make it, unfortunately, more predictable.

The saga of the "Soft South" and Southwest differs from that of the Deep South, and the explosion in "food insecurity" there is that much more surprising. Arkansas, Oklahoma, Texas, and New Mexico all post extremely bad hunger numbers, ranking them pretty close to Mississippi and Louisiana in the shame stakes. But the current bout with hunger in this region took off against a backdrop of decades of economic dynamism. Unemployment, at least until the 2008 fiscal meltdown, was low, and state economic growth was robust.

And yet, throughout the good times, economic inequalities were growing, as demonstrated by declining numbers of employees with health insurance, a rising wave of hunger, and the increasing numbers of residents who told researchers they had to choose between buying gas, paying utility bills, getting medical care, paying rent or mortgages, and buying food for their families. By 2006, the U.S. Census Bureau estimated that 17 percent of Oklahomans were living in poverty, giving it the seventh highest poverty rate in the country. Its median household income was only 80 percent of the national average.

Increasingly, Oklahoma's economy was coming to look like a pyramid, with wealth concentrated at the top and manufacturing jobs with good pay and benefits, as well as the employment provided by small family farms, being replaced by low-paying service sector work without benefits. It was the sort of societal edifice that would have been familiar to denizens of the two nineteenth-century social systems: the commercial and industrial model that created the fortunes of the Vanderbilts, Carnegies, and Rockefellers alongside tenement slums, sweatshops, and deadly work conditions in factories; and the agricultural model of Dixie, with an aristocratic elite propped up by the labor of slaves and sharecroppers. In 1979, Oklahoma's rural poverty rate was 16.5 percent; almost thirty years later, despite the country as a whole being far wealthier, it had risen to nearly 20 percent. In many counties, one in four residents was now officially listed as living below the poverty line.

A similar story held to the north, in Idaho. Tina Rojas, her elderly husband, Ruben, and Tina's three teenage children lived in an old trailer on the outskirts of the little town of Homedale. Years earlier, Ruben worked at a potato processing facility, where he made fairly decent money. But then it closed down. The family was reduced to field and orchard work, picking cherries, peaches, plums, asparagus, and onions. In a good week, their combined labor brought home somewhere in the region of four hundred dollars. More often they earned far less. When Tina and Ruben needed extra money, they pawned their van, and then painstakingly redeemed it at 25 percent interest over the next several months.

When I met them, Ruben had recently been diagnosed with a stomach tumor. Lacking health insurance but not poor enough for Medicaid, the family hadn't been able to cobble together the estimated ten thousand dollars for an operation. And so the tumor stayed in Ruben's belly. He was getting sicker, and work was becoming harder.

Tina, like an increasing number of low-income Americans, grew vegetables out back of her trailer. When the electricity was periodically cut off because the bills hadn't been paid, she cooked for her family atop an old iron potbelly stove in the cluttered living room. She longed for a big enough freezer to store the produce she grew, so the family could eat cheaply throughout the winter when no money was coming in from field work. Yet even a secondhand freezer cost close to two hundred dollars and, for the Rojas, that price tag might as well have been a million. And so, when the money ran low, they watched warily as their food supplies dwindled down to nothing. "If it wasn't for the pantries, we wouldn't be getting through the month," Tina admitted. "It tides us over for the last two weeks of the month—a good seventy-five to eighty dollars of food. Bread, cans of corn."

For agricultural workers in the region, such experiences were strung like beads along the stories of their lives. In the spring of 2005, Leora, a mother of five, visited her doctor in Caldwell. She was eight months pregnant and the doctor worried that she was malnourished. That was important not only because failing to eat properly would sap Leora of energy, but also because a rash of recent medical studies had shown that babies born to malnourished women were at particular risk of developing, over the course of their lives, hypertension, heart disease, diabetes, and thyroid problems. Insufficient iron intake in utero and during early childhood had also been linked to low IQ levels and poor academic performance in schoolchildren. "Fetal malnutrition can lead to structural or functional changes in utero that permanently increase susceptibility to chronic diseases," wrote the editors of the prestigious *British Medical Journal* in October 1997. Leora knew that she wasn't eating right, but she also realized she didn't have many options for improving her diet. "I told him, 'Well, when the summer starts I'll eat better.'" Of course, by then her child would have already been born and the health damage inflicted.

Leora was a U.S. citizen, but her husband was living in the country illegally. In the summer months—the months Leora told her doctor she would be able to eat more—the whole family worked in the fields, picking beets and other crops from dawn to dusk for a handful of dollars an hour. Leora had grown up doing this work, her parents moving between Idaho and Arizona. It was the life she knew best. During the down months, she picked up some extra cash packaging and distributing the local phone book or looking after a friend's baby during the days. Her husband worked as a construction laborer, taking low-paying jobs from subcontractors who knew not to ask questions about his immigration status. Leora, who had recently been diagnosed as bipolar, estimated that they brought in, through their labor, about $1,500 each month, supplemented at times by food stamps and her disability checks. No matter how hard they worked, they couldn't escape the all-consuming poverty; there was no way a family as large as theirs could survive on what they earned.

They lived in a $70,000 three-bedroom house on a quiet residential block twenty miles from Boise, for which they had scrabbled together the $1,500 down payment; but by 2005, well before the subprime mortgage debacle sent millions of homeowners into foreclosure, paying the $700 monthly mortgage payment was pushing them to the wall. When they fell behind after having to spend precious dollars on an operation for Leora's sister, they rented out one of the three bedrooms to a cousin. It turned out to be a mixed blessing. Yes, they had more money, but because of that extra income the government temporarily stopped giving the family food stamps, forcing Leora to choose between relying on charity and not eating. And so, reluctantly, the family fell back on the largesse of the Rescue Mission, a Christian missionary group with offices in downtown Boise that tallied both the number of meals volunteers handed out and the "decisions for Christ" taken by its clients.

"I don't eat so that they can eat," Leora said of her five children and her sister's two children, who were also living with them. "They have to eat everything on their plate. Everything. Nothing can be left. If they leave it, we eat it. They get an apple, they have to split it three ways. We limit them from eating here in the morning unless it's oatmeal or cream of wheat. If I don't make that, they eat at school. The kids drink evaporated milk. It's forty cents a can. Dinner is normally rice, beans. Every day. Rice and beans and *sopa*."

In contrast to Oklahoma and Idaho, the states that have managed to buck the hunger trends—including Connecticut, Delaware,

Hawaii, Massachusetts, Minnesota, New Hampshire, New Jersey, North Dakota, and Virginia—are generally those that have intervened more assertively on health-care access, heating subsidies for the poor, and the minimum wage. By contrast, Oklahoma and Idaho have failed to intervene; as a result, they have seen increasing numbers of residents come to rely on food stamps and private food charities to subsidize their wages. The laissez-faire capitalism that has allowed the growth of extreme deprivation among the working poor has, paradoxically, made state and state-backed charitable handouts a core part of the social contract in these regions of America.

When the Dust Bowl destroyed the Great Plains, a tidal wave of desperate, poor, rural farm laborers descended on California. John Steinbeck famously wrote about them in *Grapes of Wrath*; Dorothea Lange immortalized the visual contours of their tragedy with her camera.

Despite being mocked, and often beaten, by California's residents, who feared the migrants would take their jobs or, at the very least, lower their wages; despite being housed in disease-ridden tent cities; despite being fired if they so much as voiced support for trade unions to counter the brutal labor practices that governed California agriculture; still the desperate Oklahomans streamed into the Golden State. "How can you frighten a man whose hunger is not only in his own cramped stomach but in the wretched bellies of his children?" Steinbeck asked his readers. "You can't scare him—he has known a fear beyond every other."

Three generations on, the unincorporated, hidden shantytowns of California's Central Valley remain. Off the main roads, without signposts, not even listed on road maps, they exist yet don't exist; real people eke out their lives in these communities, but they get no services—no streetlights, no safe drinking water, sometimes not even electricity. Like similar communities in Texas, Arizona, and New Mexico, like Haitian villages amid the Florida sugarcane

fields and migrant townships in the Georgian countryside, they
have perfected the sad art of invisibility. Their populace is no longer
white, and no longer made up of onetime residents of Oklahoma.
Nowadays it is brown, and almost entirely composed of onetime
inhabitants of Mexico, pushed off the land in their home country,
forced by economic conditions outside of their control to look for
the means of survival north of the border. They know they'll find
it, because Americans demand cheap food, and keeping food cheap
means paying farm laborers abysmally, which generally means that
if you're willing enough (in other words, sufficiently desperate)
to be exploited, you'll find plenty of employers willing to do the
exploiting.

And so they arrive, legally or illegally, every day, sleeping on floors
and in garages at the homes of friends and relatives until they can
scrabble together enough dollars through backbreaking work out
in the fields to rent their own homes. English has been replaced by
Spanish and a smattering of indigenous languages from southern
Mexico. The bluegrass and folk songs of the "Okies"—as Califor-
nians derisively termed the Dust Bowl migrants —has given way to
Oaxacan *chilena*. But, despite the differences, a vein of poverty and
hunger connects past and present here. When the sun sinks below
the horizon, *colonias* like Tonyville, Lindsay, and Plainview still
fade into nothingness, their broken-down trailers and jerry-rigged
wooden houses mere blackness against the unlit dirt streets and
endless geometrically patterned orchards. And, as often as not, men,
women, and children, working the most productive agricultural
region on earth, still go to bed with bellies empty. "Sometimes we
eat one time a day," a migrant living in a tumbledown trailer with
her grandmother, mother, husband, and three children told me. She
and the rest of her family were wearing filthy thrift-store clothing,
and all except the grandmother looked deeply, painfully unhealthy.
"Beans, [nopales] cactus, water. Sometimes we ask friends for money.
We go to food pantries. We get beans, rice, some cookies, and some

vegetables. No milk. Pasta. No bread. Sometimes Jell-O. Sometimes frozen food—taquitos, enchiladas."

"You send a child off to school with a few beans wrapped in a tortilla, it's not too good," said Graciella Martinez, an organizer with the Visalia chapter of the American Friends Service Committee. "There's hunger in the land of plenty."

Plainview is twenty miles northeast of Visalia, a cute historic town deep within the Central Valley farm belt. To get to Plainview, you drive down the highway, past the mansions of Exeter, a ritzy community of local landowners where homes sell for over $250,000. You turn onto several small, unmarked roads, head into the citrus orchards, and suddenly you stumble into Plainview. It's a dusty town, the buildings ranging from broken-down shacks to cramped, but decent, wooden homes, most of which shelter perhaps twice as many people as could comfortably dwell in a two- or three-bedroom house. Seven, eight, sometimes twelve people; three, even four generations with a few hundred square feet to call their own. Many of the gardens surrounding the dwellings are home to chickens, goats, and, increasingly, small vegetable patches.

When I visited Plainview, a couple thousand people were living there, many, though by no means all, illegal immigrants. There was one food store in town, a vastly overpriced place run by a Pakistani family, who had somehow ended up in the middle of nowhere in California's Central Valley. The place was decorated with large posters advertising crates of beer for sale. Some of the residents, I was told, drove elsewhere, looking for better deals in supermarkets in towns like Visalia, or, further north, Fresno; but recently the combination of high gas prices and increased highway patrol and Immigration and Customs Enforcement (ICE) activity had scared many residents off the roads. They drove to work in the fields and back; other than that, they stayed in Plainview, trying to remain as invisible as possible. A similar fear of the immigration authorities also stopped many locals from signing on for WIC or food stamps for their U.S.-born children. It didn't matter how many times community organizers told them the food agencies weren't border enforcers; they didn't want to risk any encounters with authorities. California, like many states, fingerprinted and photographed food stamp applicants, further feeding in to the idea that a request for state aid would quickly bring you and your family to the attention of ICE agents.

And so, they bit their tongues and ponied up nearly four dollars for a dozen eggs or five dollars for a gallon of milk for the kids. If they didn't look at the sell-by dates, as often as not they'd end up with cans of beans or vegetables that should have been eaten, or thrown out, long ago. And if they ran out of dough to buy these delicacies, well, they could always cash their paychecks at the store— for a price.

Almost to a person, the adults of Plainview, those with legal residency and those still in the shadows, worked in the fields. Nowadays, in 2008, they earned eight dollars an hour, minus the mandatory Social Security deduction, and many of the workers were spending upward of one hundred dollars a week on gas driving scores of miles from Plainview to the orange and olive groves and fields of blueberries far down the valley. Those who didn't spend their days in the fields and orchards were either too old or too sick. Many had wrecked their backs over decades of agricultural work. "I was at the very top of an olive tree picking olives, and the tree trunk was rotten and broke," recalled fifty-nine-year-old widow Domitila Lemus, describing the accident that ended her thirty-five years of field labor. "I fell over and got hurt. For five minutes I was passed out. I fell on top of my bucket, and the ladder and then the tree fell on top of me." At the time, Lemus was earning thirty dollars a day, occasionally as much as fifty dollars. Now she survived, barely, on a few hundred dollars a month in disability, money that no longer stretched to cover the rising cost of food. "Meat is expensive. Milk. Beans and rice. Everything. Onions. Tomatoes. You buy less, or figure out some way to get more money." But that was easier said than done. When the money ran out, she relied on neighbors and friends quietly bringing her boxes of food. "God is big," she said softly. "Somebody always comes through." Others had had their lungs crippled by Valley Fever, the feared local disease spread by spores in the soil around Plainview.

During the picking season, a Plainview resident working six or seven days a week might bring in three hundred, even four hundred dollars weekly. It was a pittance, but at least it let them pay their rent and put a little bit of food on the table. During the fallow months, though, those long, damp times from September to May when work was scarce and competition for the few available jobs intense, their well of money would run dry. Few locals had bank accounts, let alone credit cards. Some of the more financially ambitious banded together into *tandas*—communal saving pools into which everyone contributed a monthly sum, with the proceeds being given to a different member each month. If you were a member of a *tanda*, you didn't mess about; failure to pay your dues resulted in communal shaming, or worse. In small towns, you can't really hide from a large group of angry neighbors to whom you owe money. And so, somehow, you scrabbled and scrimped, and, come hell or high water, once a month you deposited your dues with the *tanda* chair. If you were lucky enough to be in one of these pools, you might survive the winter months through collecting a lump sum and spreading it over the lean times. If you couldn't get into a *tanda*, if you hadn't established the bonds of trust that were the informal economy's equivalent of a high Equifax credit rating, you'd probably have to fall back on local loan sharks, pawnshops, and pantries.

In the winter of 2006–2007, a cold spell put a frost over the land and the orange crop was destroyed. Nobody could find employment. Badly constructed local water pipes ruptured and homes flooded, adding to the misery. One family after another ran out of money and then food. People still remember those times with terror.

"I spent the winter without turning my gas on and made do with blankets," Domitila said. Her friend, Trina, tried to rustle up a little heat by turning on her kitchen stove for an hour each night before she curled up in bed. It didn't work. She got so cold she ended up with pneumonia, as did many of her neighbors.

On the unmarked main street, a young lady, prematurely aged, lived with her five children in a small bungalow with cracked, dirty, orange-painted walls. Her husband had left long ago. The windows of the house were broken, cardboard filling in where the glass once was. A basketball hoop, the net more hole than mesh, dominated the front driveway. A red pickup truck was parked out back, loaded up with beer cans for recycling. The occupant of the house was thirty-five years old; she'd lived in Plainview seven years, since migrating north from the Mexican state of Michoacán.

"I work in the fields. Right now, we're picking cherries," she said, a mouth of faux-gold teeth catching the sun as she spoke. "I work from five o'clock in the morning. In a good week, I earn about three hundred ten dollars. About eight dollars an hour. Sometimes they pay six, sometimes ten." One of her children was born in the United States, and she received sixty-six dollars a month in food stamps for that child. (Throughout the region, families are part-legal, part-illegal. All too often, entire families will end up trying to survive, during the lean winter months, on the benefits provided the children born stateside.) At nights, to bring in extra money, she'd sometimes take shifts in a chicken-packing plant. It meant grueling hours: get up at three thirty, prepare a meager breakfast to be left for the kids when they woke up, in the car by four forty and the fields shortly after five. Pick fruit until four in the afternoon, come home, kiss the kids, head out to the plant, package chickens till midnight. And then, somehow, try to snatch a couple hours rest. Do that too long, something's liable to snap.

And at the end of the day, she still had literally no savings to weather the bad times. "During the big freeze, that was really bad. There was no work and very little to feed the children. We needed blankets. I went to Pro Diaz [an employment training program], but they didn't help. There was a long time without food." Even the pantries in the towns of Lindsay and Porterville turned her away because she didn't have a driver's license or other proof of identity. For three weeks, the family lived on little more than hope, the food stamps provided her one child, and a few cans given her in pity by a woman who usually looked after her younger kids while she worked in the fields. Finally, her church pastor lent the family money to buy food.

"My children would ask me 'Mommy, how come you're not sitting down to eat?' I'd say 'I'm not hungry.' But there wasn't enough to go around. I felt very bad. I cried a lot. When my oldest son found out, I said I was desperate because I couldn't find a job. But I never told him it was because I didn't know where I'd get money to feed them."

In nearby Lindsay, Santiago, his heavily pregnant new wife Benita, and their children by previous marriages were, if possible, even hungrier. Santiago had had an accident twelve years earlier and could no longer work in the fields. So he made a few dollars here and there by recycling cans that he and his kids would pick up on the street, building fences, and occasionally cleaning houses. When the stars aligned, the Mixteco- and Spanish-speaking migrant could earn $250 in a week; more often, he'd end up with $100 and change. The adults never ate dinner and rarely had breakfast. For them, lunch, cooked on a stove set up under a canopy in the fly-infested backyard, was their one meal. Rice, beans, and tortillas every day. And if stomachs growled in outrage later on, caught in limbo hours from the last meal and hours more until the next, well, they'd just pull their belts tighter and try to choke off the acidic pain.

Do you have milk in the house?
No. Never.

Orange Juice?
Nada.

Meat?
No. Never. Except Sunday.

Breakfast?
The children, they have breakfast in the school. Me? Nothing.

Do you get hungry?
Yes.

What does it feel like?
I feel sad, and mean and frustrated. Because when I don't have work, I want to go to work just for food.

About weekends, Santiago's six-year-old, Samuel, added simply, "We eat not so much. At class we get lunch. Not over here."

Even in Fresno, the largest city of the Central Valley, similar stories held. For the agricultural laborers who lived in town and drove into the peach orchards to work, life was a continual juggling act. Buy food or pay for gas? Shoes for the kids or keep the electricity running? Insurance or rent or milk for the baby? "Two days ago, Javier was very upset because there was nothing to eat," a woman with a diseased, bloodied left eye, numb hands, and dangerously high blood pressure said of her young son after the family ran dry. "I don't have anything. Only a little bit of chicken. One gallon of milk—and I'm trying to manage it because every day my youngest child has to have a cup of milk. The check my husband is getting today is going toward the rent. I don't know what we're going to do. I was just asking my husband. He said he was going to try to get a check in advance so he could pay the insurance and get a little bit of food."

In schools like Lowell Elementary, in the poor neighborhoods, 100 percent of the students were eligible for free lunches. "We eat two times a day. Breakfast and lunch. For dinner, sometimes the children will eat a bowl of cereal after school. Nothing afterward," one woman asserted tearfully. Her nine-year-old son, Hector, a small boy in a striped orange T-shirt, black shorts, and sneakers, dreamt of eating meat, but, he said, his voice a whisper, his evening meal was "Frosted Flakes, with milk. At four o'clock. When I come to school, I come to the cafeteria. They give me breakfast. Burritos. Cereal. On weekends, I eat fruit. For dinner, cereal." For a treat, his parents would take him and his siblings to McDonald's. He was allowed to get a double cheeseburger, no fries. His mom and dad would sit and watch while the children ate.

There is a stereotype that these people of the Central Valley are lazy, that they are in the United States to steal "American jobs" or to mooch off the public purse. Like most stereotypes, it's ugly and it's false. In fact, they work extraordinarily hard, doing low-wage, body-destroying jobs that few homegrown Americans have shown much inclination for in recent decades. They work because they want to send money home to family in Mexico and to ensure their children thrive in the United States. Despite the grind of their daily lives, in some ways they are among the most fervent of believers in the American Dream. They also work because the alternative is unthinkable. Here illegally, they cannot access food stamps and other government services. If they don't work, they don't have money; and if they don't have money, they go from their already meager one or two meals a day to none.

Perhaps that's why the tomato pickers of Immokalee, Florida, a small community northwest of the Everglades, continued to pick fruit for companies like McDonald's, Taco Bell, and Burger King, despite earning only forty-five cents for every thirty pounds of tomatoes. They hadn't had a pay raise in years, and inflation had utterly eroded the value of their wages. They earned, on average, ten thousand dollars a year out in the fields, meaning they were trapped below the government-defined poverty line. But they had nowhere else to go, and so they stayed at their jobs despite the humbling conditions. Perhaps that's why they continued to pick for Burger King even after Burger King refused to sign on to a 2005 agreement that raised the rate by a penny a pound, potentially adding a few thousand dollars a year to the migrant workers' earnings at the negligible cost to a company like Burger King of three hundred thousand dollars annually. Perhaps that's why they kept picking the tomatoes even after Burger King signed on in mid-2008—when faced with the possibility of a consumer boycott campaign—but the Florida Tomato Growers' Exchange, representing the people who owned the land on which the tomatoes were grown, blocked the pay increase, and the money instead went into an escrow account. They worked for scandalously low wages not out of any particular love for tomatoes, or for the growers on whose land they toiled, but because they didn't have any real alternatives. They were peculiarly vulnerable, pawns in a game that they could not win.

Despite the efforts of Cesar Chavez's United Farm Workers union in California a generation ago, and notwithstanding the campaigns elsewhere of local groups such as the Coalition of Immokalee Workers, most farm laborers in America remain nonunionized. They are generally paid by the pound of crop harvested, or by the hour, rather than signing on for an annual salary. At harvest time, they might work eighty hours a week. During the wintertime, they often go months with no income. And they almost never receive benefits; they don't qualify for unemployment, they have limited access to Social Security, and employer-provided health insurance is about as common as verified sightings of the Yeti.

When organizers working with these laborers call for food stamps and other benefits to be made available to them, critics say "illegals" should be sent home, that U.S. taxpayers shouldn't subsidize the hordes of undocumented migrants who have come north in recent years. Yet when states periodically get tough on their undocumented populations—as Arizona and Colorado did in the latter years of the Bush presidency, giving police officers powers to check on people's immigration status, and restricting access to social services—their farmers, who have long played a don't-ask-don't-tell game around the immigration status of their employees, end up navigating roiling waters. The fact is, there are many illegal residents in places like Plainview and Lindsay at least in part because the employers and landowners have, for generations, benefited from these plausible deniability arrangements. They don't ask whether their workers are illegal; but they pay them low enough wages and preside over bad enough working environments that there's a pretty good chance that most of those who stay the course lack other, legal, employment options.

When Arizona and Colorado cracked down on their "illegal aliens," farmers quickly faced labor shortages and unharvested fields. In Pueblo, Colorado, in 2007, landowners even began hiring low-security prisoners, who came to work escorted by armed prison guards, to harvest their sweet corn, peppers, and melons, because, in the absence of a migratory and illegal population, no one else was willing to work for the wages they could offer.

Given these realities, it is entirely unfair to also cut off access to basic food provision mechanisms to these vulnerable laborers. In the long term, legislators need to mandate higher wages for farmworkers as a way to integrate the industry into the broader, regulated economy. In the short term, given the prevalence of undocumented workers in America's fields and packing houses, food stamps and other welfare programs need to be made accessible to them. If we, as a society, can tolerate eating fast-food burgers kept cheap by the fact that undocumented, underpaid workers picked the lettuce, tomatoes, and onions that sit atop the beef patties—which were also most likely processed at a slaughterhouse by other men and women living in the twilight of illegality—surely we can also tolerate a more inclusive safety net for those workers and their children.

Back East, in the Dust Bowl, the land has dried up once again. Over the past decade many farms have failed, farmers have taken government money to put the land back to grass, and residents have, once more, fallen on hard times.

Melrose, in the flat eastern plateau of New Mexico, an hour's drive east of where the earth goes crazy and the majestic desert rears up out of canyons and arroyos, is a small place. Going at the speed limit, it takes twenty-eight seconds to get from the east side of town to the west. But in that half minute you can look around and see the signs that it is dying. A half century ago, the town was dominated by several soaring grain elevators; its roads were clogged by lines of trucks coming in with grain; its main street was bustling; and the farmers, who had bought land at five dollars an acre, along with the cowboys, would come in on weekends to whoop it up in Melrose's restaurants and saloons. Nowadays it has a school—some of whose two hundred-plus students are so poor their parents can't afford to buy shoes and winter coats for them, and at least thirty of whom now routinely arrive in the mornings hungry, according to school nutritionist Carol Moore; a senior center, where the town's elderly come for free food and company, buoyed by a sign that reads "Life isn't about waiting for the storm to pass. It's about learning to dance in the rain"; a food pantry; and four churches. Other than that, the life has gone out of Melrose.

"I never went hungry in my life," said seventy-seven-year-old great-grandmother R. I. Campbell fiercely. R. I. had no first names; her granddaddy, who named her, wanted a boy baby; when a girl was born, a couple years before the soil turned to dust, the disappointed old man simply gave her the initials to the names he had set aside for his hoped-for male heir.

R. I., who was a living encyclopedia of health problems, was essentially homebound; she was living out her days in a small house on the edge of town, its heavily carpeted living room cluttered with family photos, a small piano, a carved wooden buffalo head, and other trinkets, as well as an oxygen tank, a hydraulic chair that literally lifted her from sitting to upright position when she needed to stand, and miscellaneous other medical equipment. When she left her home, it was to be driven to the doctor's or, briefly, to the pantry.

"We might not have had the most expensive food, but we always had plenty at the table. I milked a cow for the first time when I was four or five years old, had a Jersey cow just as gentle as could be. My sister sat on one side, I sat on the other, we each had a gallon bucket, and we milked. Now I live on Social Security and I go to our food pantry. I am very grateful we have the food pantry. Like I say, I don't eat high on the hog, but I always get plenty to eat. Of course, I [also] get food from the Salvation Army."

R. I. could no longer afford to buy meat or fresh fruit juice. With no savings, she lived on $791.60 a month in Social Security—her legacy from working two decades at a local bank until she had to quit in 1985 after being diagnosed with cancer. And out of that pittance she had to spend more than two hundred dollars a month supplementing her Medicare insurance; she had so many medical problems that without the top-up insurance she couldn't have afforded the 20 percent co-pays under Medicare for doctors' visits. Even with the additional insurance, she still had to spend five dollars on each generic prescription drug and ten dollars on the nongenerics; and because she took so many drugs the numbers quickly added up.

"I wasn't raised with having to have steak and expensive things to eat. I was raised on beans and potatoes and cornbread. Of course, we had butter and cheese and cottage cheese, and hogs and beef, and what we couldn't eat we canned. I used to raise a big garden and can. I'm not able to do that now." She stopped and laughed. "Might be a good thing. I couldn't afford the water bill." As R. I. talked of the processed foods from the pantry that she, and most of her friends, now survived on, the old lady's past welled up in her sickroom. "I don't eat as good as I did when I was a kid on the farm. Mother cooked all the time—even cooked for the school; made hot rolls every day for the school. We had lots of vegetables. We didn't have any fruit trees, but some of the neighbors did, and we canned fruit. We had a sweet thing every meal. I like pies, I like jelly."

"We opened our little pantry June 18th of this year [2008]," said

Don Smith's friend, Hank Jordan. "The first day we were open we gave out twenty food boxes. This past Wednesday [two months after the pantry opened] we gave out fifty-one. If fifty-one people came to our pantry, and the population of our town is seven hundred fifty, that's quite a percentage. That's fifty-one boxes, upwards of one hundred twenty people."

Conclusion: After the Fall

"WE LEARN FROM HISTORY that we learn nothing from history," George Bernard Shaw once wrote. That is the modern world's blessing and its curse. We have, in profound ways, liberated ourselves from our pasts by ignoring the constraints imposed by those pasts. In the process we have unlocked many of the mysteries of science, extended our life spans, created ways of traveling, communicating, and sharing information and knowledge that our forefathers could not even have dreamt of. We have made our societies materially wealthier and held out the promise of endless, technology-driven quality-of-life advances. Yet we have also developed a startling shell of hubris. So convinced are we of our special natures, of our difference from those who came before, that we tend to dismiss the lessons of history.

From the time of the Wall Street crash of October 1929 through the 1930s, industrial economies the world over imploded under the weight of massive debt, overleveraged banks, and bursting get-rich-quick stock bubbles. The go-go twenties, years in which America surged to economic preeminence, its government taking a backseat to the dynamic corporations that made up the spine of its private sector, gave way to more than a decade of economic crisis, followed by a world war. For the lucky, for those who held private sector jobs or picked up work on government-funded infrastructure projects, these were years of scarcity and angst. For the unlucky, they brought destitution, hunger, and—ultimately—cataclysmic bloodshed.

Three-quarters of a century later, the grandchildren and great-grandchildren of the Depression era went on a spending spree the likes of which the world had never before seen. Governments encouraged the rise of a borrowing-based consumer culture; taxes were cut, and the apparatuses of government—including regulatory agencies created during the New Deal to prevent runaway markets caroming toward hidden precipices—were denuded. Dozens of new lending systems emerged, opaque in their workings, octopus-like in their reach, all designed to ease the flow of money, to flood every nook and cranny of society with too-tempting-to-resist loans. People borrowed to buy homes and then borrowed against rising on-paper home values to pay off credit cards that they had borrowed from for years to buy consumer goods, to pay for health care, to put food on the table that their paychecks couldn't stretch to cover. The poor borrowed to stay afloat; the middle classes borrowed to keep up with the Joneses, to pad their already opulent lifestyles. Investment companies borrowed to buy bundles of mortgages from banks that they hoped to be able to turn a quick buck on. Governments borrowed to pay for wars and domestic programs that they wanted to pursue but didn't want to have to pay for through increasing tax burdens on their electorates.

Huge sums of money circulated around the global financial arteries at ever-increasing speed. Temporarily, vast amounts of wealth were, indeed, unleashed. And then, as happened in the late 1920s, the various bubbles upon which the whole edifice floated began to pop.

Unnoticed by the still-partying majority, an increasing number of poor people ran out of credit options and started cutting down on everything from gasoline for their cars to food for their kids. Then, lower-middle-class homeowners began to default on their mortgages and home equity loans, and suddenly the crowd still partying got markedly smaller. The institutions that had lent all this money out in the first place began to collapse, as did the stock portfolios and retirement accounts of millions of members of the global middle class. And the governments that had stood back for decades and watched the whole scene unfold found that they had to dig deep into their reserves to inject startling amounts of cash—trillions of dollars all told—back into the crippled financial system. When push came to shove, by late 2008 the economic model pursued by American policy makers for a generation—and implemented not just in the United States but in many countries on many continents—had failed almost as spectacularly as did the institutions and political assumptions of pre-1929 America.

What replaces that discredited system, what new social compact emerges between the government, the citizenry, and the business community, is still up in the air. Can America regain its reputation as a true land of opportunity? Can it feed its hungry and provide jobs to its idled millions? Can it put in place living-wage laws so that the Aubretia Edicks dotted around the country no longer have to consider eggs a luxury; so that the Becky Darnalls don't have to supplement their wages with visits to church pantries; so that the Rosie Kerrs don't have to borrow from family members to buy gas to drive to work and to purchase food to feed their kids? Can America resume its historical role as the shining city on a hill?

"It matters little if you have the right to sit at the front of the bus if you can't afford the bus fare," then-presidential hopeful Barack Obama told his audience at a meeting of the National Association for the Advancement of Colored People (NAACP) in July 2008. "It matters little if you have the right to sit at the lunch counter if you can't afford the lunch. So long as Americans are denied the decent wages, and good benefits, and fair treatment they deserve, the dream for which so many gave so much will remain out of reach."

America's forty-fourth president has inherited an extraordinary crisis. Only once in the past century, when Franklin Roosevelt took the oath of office in 1933, has an incoming administration faced such dismal economic prospects. And as with Roosevelt's New Deal program, so Obama's promises to reinvigorate the American economy and breathe new life into the American Dream will have to be judged over the course of years rather than months. Elected in 1932, it took until the late 1930s before Roosevelt managed to put all his signature economic programs—Social Security, unemployment insurance, a minimum wage—in place. Winning the presidential election in 2008, Obama's administration will be cleaning up fallout from the Bush-era meltdown well into the next decade.

During the election campaign and in the transitional period that followed, Obama's economic advisers proposed a temporary moratorium on home foreclosures; they advocated increasing the minimum wage up to a point close to the "living wage" threshold identified by economists such as Bob Pollin; and they pushed for various publicly funded infrastructure programs designed both to limit the unemployment caused by collapsing investment and consumption spending and also to remake America as a green economy.

All of these ideas are good starts. But they are only starts. For Obama, there is both the need and the opportunity to embrace as comprehensive a set of institutional changes as those that, collectively, came to make up Roosevelt's New Deal. Over the next several years, tax systems will have to be rewritten to tackle the country's growing income gaps. Health-care delivery systems need to be created to ensure that the poor and near-poor no longer have to risk hunger and destitution to pay their medical bills when they get sick. Fuel and food subsidy programs will have to be expanded and, in some cases, created from scratch. And the government will need to start looking at how best to make long-term investments to build up the nation's stock of affordable housing for those driven out of the private market and beggared by the foreclosure crisis. Unemployment insurance will have to be updated to ensure coverage for job-hopping, service-sector employees. And private pension systems will have to be shored up, with the state providing incentives to companies to expand, rather than renege on, their pension obligations to longtime workers.

More generally, workers on the lower rungs of the economic ladder have to be better protected, as they are in most other wealthy nations, from the vagaries of everyday life. The Family Medical Leave Act needs to be updated so that part-time workers and those in small businesses can take paid leave to look after sick relatives. A federal version of laws passed recently in San Francisco, Washington, D.C., and Milwaukee, which grant a limited number of paid sick days to all employees, should be implemented. And—as is already the case in most other wealthy democracies—Congress should speedily pass a Federal Employees Paid Parental Leave Act, granting four weeks of paid leave to parents of newborn and newly adopted children.

To help companies meet these extra costs, corporate tax structures will need to be modified to provide partial tax rebates to smooth the implementation of these new rules.

At the state level, lawmakers ought to enact their own versions of the successful federal Earned Income Tax Credit program, which uses tax rebates as a way to cycle more money back into the pockets of low-paid workers and then through the local economy.

Taken as a whole, these proposals would, over the course of the Obama presidency, move the country toward a new social compact based around what Rosemary Harris, communications director of 9to5, National Association of Working Women, termed the principle of "economic justice." As important, channeling money toward low-income Americans would provide a massive long-term stimulus to a contracting economy.

These programs will cost money, in a period in which government funds are increasingly stretched thin. But, as the Nobel Prize–winning economist and *New York Times* columnist Paul Krugman has repeatedly noted, when faced with an economic implosion of the magnitude currently confronting America, it becomes not just acceptable but imperative to temporarily increase government deficit spending to keep the broader economy afloat. Absent such spending, absent creative, aggressive intervention from the Federal government, there is a real risk that the economy will shrink dramatically over many years and the numbers of destitute Americans will continue to soar.

For Don Smith, the hunger stalking America in 2008 represented a crisis of biblical proportions. "You serve somebody when they come in that door and look them straight in the eye. You can see their soul. The Book says 'Feed my people.' You've got to feed your people. 'When I was in prison, you came to visit me. When I was unclothed you clad me. When I was hungry you fed me.' If we don't get anything else done in this world, at least you helped your fellow man."

Index

About the Author

Sasha Abramsky is an award-winning magazine writer and book author. His work has appeared in the *Atlantic Monthly*, *Mother Jones*, the *Nation*, the *London Guardian* and many other publications. He is a senior fellow at Demos and teaches in the writing program at the University of California at Davis. Abramsky lives in Sacramento, California with his wife and two children.

Other Books from PoliPointPress

The Blue Pages: A Directory of Companies Rated by Their Politics and Practices

Helps consumers match their buying decisions with their political values by listing the political contributions and business practices of over one thousand companies. $9.95, paperback.

Rose Aguilar, *Red Highways: A Liberal's Journey into the Heartland*

Challenges red state stereotypes to reveal new strategies for progressives. $15.95, paperback.

Dean Baker, *Plunder and Blunder: The Rise and Fall of the Bubble Economy*

Chronicles the growth and collapse of the stock and housing bubbles and explains how policy blunders and greed led to the catastrophic—but completely predictable—market meltdowns. $15.95, paperback.

Jeff Cohen, *Cable News Confidential: My Misadventures in Corporate Media*

Offers a fast-paced romp through the three major cable news channels—Fox, CNN, and MSNBC—and delivers a serious message about their failure to cover the most urgent issues of the day. $14.95, paperback.

Marjorie Cohn, *Cowboy Republic: Six Ways the Bush Gang Has Defied the Law*

Shows how the executive branch under President Bush has systematically defied the law instead of enforcing it. $14.95, paperback.

Marjorie Cohn and **Kathleen Gilberd,** *Rules of Disengagement: The Politics and Honor of Military Dissent*

Examines what U.S. military men and women have done—and what their families and readers can do—to resist illegal wars and to respond to sexual harassment, racial discrimination, and inadequate health care. $14.95, paperback.

Joe Conason, *The Raw Deal: How the Bush Republicans Plan to Destroy Social Security and the Legacy of the New Deal*

Reveals the well-financed and determined effort to undo the Social Security Act and other New Deal programs. $11.00, paperback.

Kevin Danaher, Shannon Biggs, and **Jason Mark,** *Building the Green Economy: Success Stories from the Grassroots*

Shows how community groups, families, and individual citizens have protected their food and water, cleaned up their neighborhoods, and strengthened their local economies. $16.00, paperback.

Kevin Danaher and **Alisa Gravitz,** *The Green Festival Reader: Fresh Ideas from Agents of Change*

Collects the best ideas and commentary from some of the most forward green thinkers of our time. $15.95, paperback.

Reese Erlich, *Dateline Havana: The Real Story of U.S. Policy and the Future of Cuba*

Explores Cuba's strained relationship with the United States, the island nation's evolving culture and politics, and prospects for U.S.–Cuba policy with the departure of Fidel Castro. $22.95, hardcover.

Reese Erlich, *The Iran Agenda: The Real Story of U.S. Policy and the Middle East Crisis*

Explores the turbulent recent history between the two countries and how it has led to a showdown over nuclear technology. $14.95, paperback.

Steven Hill, *10 Steps to Repair American Democracy*

Identifies the key problems with American democracy, especially election practices, and proposes ten specific reforms to reinvigorate it. $11.00, paperback.

Markos Kounalakis and **Peter Laufer,** *Hope Is a Tattered Flag: Voices of Reason and Change for the Post-Bush Era*

Gathers together the most listened-to politicos and pundits, activists and thinkers, to answer the question: what happens after Bush leaves office? $29.95, hardcover; $16.95 paperback.

Yvonne Latty, *In Conflict: Iraq War Veterans Speak Out on Duty, Loss, and the Fight to Stay Alive*

Features the unheard voices, extraordinary experiences, and personal photographs of a broad mix of Iraq War veterans, including Congressman Patrick Murphy, Tammy Duckworth, Kelly Daugherty, and Camilo Mejia. $24.00, hardcover.

Phillip Longman, *Best Care Anywhere: Why VA Health Care Is Better Than Yours*

Shows how the turnaround at the long-maligned VA hospitals provides a blueprint for salvaging America's expensive but troubled health care system. $14.95, paperback.

Phillip Longman and **Ray Boshara,** *The Next Progressive Era*

Provides a blueprint for a re-empowered progressive movement and describes its implications for families, work, health, food, and savings. $22.95, hardcover.

Marcia and **Thomas Mitchell,** *The Spy Who Tried to Stop a War: Katharine Gun and the Secret Plot to Sanction the Iraq Invasion*

Describes a covert operation to secure UN authorization for the Iraq war and the furor that erupted when a young British spy leaked it. $23.95, hardcover.

Susan Mulcahy, ed., *Why I'm a Democrat*

Explores the values and passions that make a diverse group of Americans proud to be Democrats. $14.95, paperback.

David Neiwert, *The Eliminationists: How Hate Talk Radicalized the American Right*

Argues that the conservative movement's alliances with far-right extremists have not only pushed the movement's agenda to the right, but also have become a malignant influence increasingly reflected in political discourse. $16.95, paperback.

Christine Pelosi, *Campaign Boot Camp: Basic Training for Future Leaders*

Offers a seven-step guide for successful campaigns and causes at all levels of government. $15.95, paperback.

William Rivers Pitt, *House of Ill Repute: Reflections on War, Lies, and America's Ravaged Reputation*

Skewers the Bush Administration for its reckless invasions, warrantless wiretaps, lethally incompetent response to Hurricane Katrina, and other scandals and blunders. $16.00, paperback.

Sarah Posner, *God's Profits: Faith, Fraud, and the Republican Crusade for Values Voters*

Examines corrupt televangelists' ties to the Republican Party and unprecedented access to the Bush White House. $19.95, hardcover.

Nomi Prins, *Jacked: How "Conservatives" Are Picking Your Pocket— Whether You Voted for Them or Not*

Describes how the "conservative" agenda has affected your wallet, skewed national priorities, and diminished America—but not the American spirit. $12.00, paperback.

Cliff Schecter, *The Real McCain: Why Conservatives Don't Trust Him—And Why Independents Shouldn't*

Explores the gap between the public persona of John McCain and the reality of this would-be president. $14.95, hardcover.

Norman Solomon, *Made Love, Got War: Close Encounters with America's Warfare State*

Traces five decades of American militarism and the media's all-too-frequent failure to challenge it. $24.95, hardcover.

John Sperling et al., *The Great Divide: Retro vs. Metro America*

Explains how and why our nation is so bitterly divided into what the authors call Retro and Metro America. $19.95, paperback.

Daniel Weintraub, *Party of One: Arnold Schwarzenegger and the Rise of the Independent Voter*

Explains how Schwarzenegger found favor with independent voters, whose support has been critical to his success, and suggests that his bipartisan approach represents the future of American politics. $19.95, hardcover.

Curtis White, *The Spirit of Disobedience: Resisting the Charms of Fake Politics, Mindless Consumption, and the Culture of Total Work*

Debunks the notion that liberalism has no need for spirituality and describes a "middle way" through our red state/blue state political impasse. Includes three powerful interviews with John DeGraaf, James Howard Kunstler, and Michael Ableman. $24.00, hardcover.

For more information, please visit www.p3books.com.